Social Possibilities

Poetic Voices of Hope

Edited by

Zaneta V. Johns

Lisa Tomey-Zonneveld

Publication Date: June 2025

Raleigh, North Carolina USA

ISBN 978-1-962374-49-1 Paperback

ISBN 978-1-962374-50-7 ePub

TABLE OF CONTENTS

INTRODUCTION

Zaneta V. Johns

Social Possibilities is a literary sanctuary at a time of heightened uncertainty and distress. We assembled global poetic voices to ease our growing anxieties. We are faced with conflicting perspectives and occasional despair. This anthology is filled with thoughtful optimism. Rather than ignore the challenges facing our humanity, we lean in to acknowledge them while remaining hopeful. Poetry promotes understanding, empathy and compassion, which are crucial to bridging social and political divides. Featured poets illuminate a path to help you uphold justice. Similarly, we encourage you to challenge the status quo and not remain silent. Silence does not promote justice for the underserved. With unwavering devotion, please share your voice and light for the betterment of our global community.

This collection features poems that address themes of unity and serenity, ranging from calm to intense. From the first poem, "I Let Go," through the last poem, "Into the Light," these expressions are a compelling call to action. You will find personal insights, reassurance, and invaluable alternatives to fear and adversity. We celebrate these profound aspirations for a future of social connectedness.

It is not too late for The Beloved Community, envisioned and coined by Dr. Martin Luther King Jr. Armed with these impactful messages, let's normalize kindness as an essential initial step toward harmony.

SARFRAZ AHMED

I Let Go

I let go
Free you from my heart
Unveil the beauty
Watch it spread its wings
Take flight
Once caged
Hidden from sight

I let go
Let hope
Bring its own kind of magic
Release the burdens
Trauma holding you back
Before the attack
Spurs the violence
The bottle and the bombs

Break the walls of silence
As you go with the flow
As you close your eyes
As you begin to let go

RITA ANDERSON

Waiting Room

[*Charity Hospital, New Orleans*]

In this pit of iodine, stress, and sutures,
I am a paper flower with numbers on it.

Unaware that I could fly, I do...
right over the crowd around me,

heads down as they rifle through
recycled news, coughing up dreams.

I lift the hand of another patient, a girl
playing ball against cracks in the wall,

but her mother does not seem worried
that I have carried her off. Relieved,

perhaps, that neither of us is alone
anymore, the child and I talk in smiles,

gliding through the park, as leaves
brush against our skin like a welcome

summer rain—before we return to
the sickroom where, *renewed*, we

dip down to heal the other faces
that have taken the ceiling for sky.

Hurricane Rain, the Final Wave

For the 10th anniversary of Katrina

When the rain started that time, I welcomed
the break it would mean in the heat in
another torturous month of temps you

could do nothing with in a summer that
collected volume in the corner like cast off rags.
That night, I watched as a parade of drops

turned dust into mud in the street where we
had strolled until you were tired enough to sleep,
feverish in the teething dance that infants do

on their way to becoming toddlers. Normally,
when rain happened like this—after streetlights
spark up—the rain was an intimate that filled

a world where I was alone, a calm pulse that
let the stillness be *enough*. But it stormed
through that sleepless night and relief became

irritation. Living as we did in a city that sat
below sea level, every occupant knew we were
on "borrowed" time, the best pumping stations

in the world unable to keep up with the water
that poured in—until there was nowhere left to
displace it. And the sweet music of a falling torrent

pitched to a shriek against the roof like an
intruder hellbent on getting *inside*. When the power
went out, I held the phone to my ear until its silence

unnerved me. You slept through it, safe in an infant
cocoon of dreams,
        as I fought an impulse to wake you
and grip you to my breast,
        afraid that my fear would be

contagious, a terror that would not rest. Then,
before sunrise, when Katrina rose above the cars,
lawns flooded into a lake and a Natural Disaster

was declared, I was sure that *This was the end*.
But in the darkest moments—where neither prayer
nor tears could find me—
        there was only the joy of you,
and a wave of sadness
        that I might never see you walk

or hear your voice pick up
        the narrative of your own life story.

You Have a Poem I Want

to take a drink of, the one about a porcelain

bowl with soft blue flowers. It belongs
to an aging woman who caresses
the hand of her caretaker: It is
the gift of life, love in the room of death.

How have you been? as scenes fly past
like stations we do not stop for on our speeding
train, but I miss a mother's touch and
the sun on the heads of a field
choked with Black-Eyed Susans.

We are not doctors, but how we study
the negatives as a way to keep
the hurt from spreading. The past
is a room full of echoes where we cry
out like dogs who have been left in the rain—
and I long to learn another trade.

But, your blue bowl—like a tender touch after
the fire is gone—reminds me that I have
forgotten how to turn out the flashlight,
its beam catching the rafters of my own ribs,
my skull. A mirror I cannot escape for,

while I can *recognize* peace: the tolerance
of an egret poised next to a sleeping calf,
it is you who have found acceptance,
that prized pasture dazed with sunlight.

Yours is the steady wisdom of a nature
that has taken root, and I lack a planter's
patience, just as I know I would break
that fragile bowl of yours were it mine.

NELL ANTHONY

Socializing the Spaces

Calming the chaos. Sweeping through my world.
    Cleaning out its clutter.
Gathering goals with fans.
Pinching pennies. Adding up affirmations.
    Sharing it all with the world.

Narrative therapy. Pulling in the punches.
    Writing down the warnings.
Filling in the spaces. Telling all the truths.
Will the history be shared?
Don't be shy. Transcribe the biography.
Instructed how to reform narrative.
    We learned to rewrite trauma.

Life Lessons. Counted blessings.
My story changed over time.
    Yet, grateful to be alive.
List your gratitude. I've stated mine.

Scribing the themes of eternity.
The Earth never stopped spinning.
    The wind surrounded us.
Together, humankind and elements shared spaces.
An infinite appreciation.

Writers' helping writers. We had dreams.
They were comparable to one another.
Let's stand together. Helped edit this.
    I granted you a cover.
Did you know? Someone gave an answer.
Can you show me? Another offered instruction.
I knew an excellent editor.
    A guy in Greece does great graphics.
We worked individually, collectively,
    toward common goals.

Live, laugh, and love.
Pictures of fun-loving creatures.
    Offered glimpses into my globe.
Come laugh with me.
Tell me your dreams. Elaborate on your existence.
create alongside me.
We plastered our pix across the cybersphere.
Shared, tweeted, and insta'd
    our content across virtual worlds.

Through the atmosphere of cyber space,
    the matrix was affection.
Peace, hope, and cheers.
We filled our spaces with trivia, laughter,
    pictures, sayings and quotes
And above all positive reinforcements.
Come, participate, and leave anxiety
    at the threshold.

Stepping into Worlds

When I step into her world,
    she eagerly shares it with me.
Her quarters become mine.
    Our smiles identical and warm.
She makes me laugh.
I share my dreams with her.
She shares her woes with me.
That's her way. I accept it and all she has to say.

When we go to the market, she buys me things.
A bundle of strawberries for my happiness,
pineapple chunks for my sweet tooth.
Artichokes for my pleasure.
I purchase her greens and butter beans.
    They're her favorites.
    Most fruits are hard for her to chew.

We create a new space as we meander
    among the sellers and patrons.
We share our laughter and affection.
We tell people our stories.
Tempting them to tell us theirs.
Intermingling, no strangers met.
And it brings smiles and gleams to eyes.
We make them a part of what we have between us.

We pack up our things, carrying them to our ride,
Laugh and draw stares.
They're delighted to be a part of our social order.

Our spirits grab them close.
Hugging them, Pulling them ever nearer.
Welcoming them to laugh and play with us.
We proudly share our energy
    with those who surround us.
Our love for each other flows out into their worlds.
Inviting them to bask in our convivial hope.

The chain of encouraging warmth follows us home.
She puts away her gifts from me.
I leave her content and watching TV.
I make my way back to my own quarters.
Ready to welcome the love and strength
    she has given me throughout our day together.
Basking in the comfort of all
    we have created amongst us.
Bringing it home with me along with the market,
    shared stories, and hopeful gazes.
Ready to release the happiness, pleasure and
    feed my sweet tooth.
At last, I can rest knowing I've touched a few worlds
    along with the woman I call Mom.

One Message

Desperate to be seen.
I saw you.
Your message tossed to the masses.
Did you mean it to go so far?
Everyone sees you.

There is a truth you forgot to tell.
A moment you've yet to fulfill.
Was this deliberate?
Did you mean to break the mold?
Was this considered a goal?

Thank you for going viral.
Telling your tale.
Making us see the facts.
Helping us learn to be free.

Your time. Your sell. Your mission.
Your culture. Your smile. Your vision.
Coloring our surroundings. Filling in our creases.
Shouting we're great, we're awesome.
Despite our calamities.

We can! You say we can!
We do! Because we are told we can!

No longer desperate.
Or unseen.
You've communicated one message.
Creating a following of optimism.

NANCI ARVIZU

One starfish at a time

When I sit in the spaces
And I see the faces
And hear the words that others share

Yes, there is upset and angst
And boiling blood
That we all hear

We each speak
And let the words out
We find our way to the next space
The one where change takes place

We start by looking out
Then we look in
And suddenly
There is Hope

These are the words I hear

We want better
We'll know what to do and we will do the work
Help one person through it and find
    the other side together
Little versions of what is happening in D.C.
Less effective than I thought it would be
Recognize we have been traumatized
Love our neighbors, love our country, love ourselves

We were complicit to let this happen
I hope more people open their eyes
Not enough dot connecting
Can we learn from collapse?
Can we reshape our ideals in a new way?
We've been in denial for too long
You can't affect others until you affect yourself
The time is always right to do what is right *
Teach love
Respect yourself, respect others
What can I do?
I can touch one life at a time
I can do better
Be a starfish

* Dr. Martin Luther King Jr.

DAVID B. BARNES

My Private World

"What," he asked, "is making you smile so?"
He asked this as he came from the woods
    to walk beside me on a mountain trail.
Never breaking stride,
    never frowning at the interruption
I said, "Well stranger,
    what is here that would prevent a smile?
Pointing to the left
    we saw wild turkey hens and their young.
He walked along beside me
    dodging small dogwood and hickory limbs.
I looked up at the sound
    of a woodpecker looking for food.
We walked on at a leisurely pace.
Orange, yellow, green butterflies and moths
    wove in and out of our stroll.
Fir and flower were constant companions
    as a breeze filled the gap
    between us and the trees.
We each cupped our hands over our ears
    to better hear songbirds
    and my favorite woods sound of all:
    Fast water breaking over age old rocks.
My mind's eye saw white water and trout swimming.
Without turning I said,
    "This is my private world that
    you may now share."

He patted my arm.
"I thank you. My day was bright
    but not as cheery as it is now.
"You have a fine private world."
He walked back into the woods whistling.
I come here to empty my worries into the woods.
I come here to open my heart.
I come here to become whole.

NAYANJYOTI BARUAH

Happiness

Here and there happiness is,
But no one recognizes where it is.
Every day everyone runs after it, but
Almost everyone knows not what it is.

Happiness is found high and low;
But it's not good to go and purchase from the store.
One great outlook requires for
Seeing, smelling, feeling, and finding it.
Farmers smell it in the paddy field,
Rickshaw men find it in the full passenger's seat,
Pregnant women feel it after giving birth to a baby,
When wage labours always get paid in the evening.

Let's surrender ourselves at our work,
And struggle to achieve it, score it.
So, let us steal not others' happiness
Until we deserve it.

ROBERTA BATORSKY

Pashtun Sanwich

For Rebecca

Two footfalls past fences
the military base's landscape
abruptly changes,
revealing multitudes of humans
trudging in ceaseless,
ancient migration
on quiet, anxious lines
which file past tents inflated to capacity
where vaccines await arms.

Dark eyes blink over masks and
flowy hijabs stir without wind.
Women and babes in
colors from another world
radiate pain and disruption and
no language suffices to ease the transition
or relieve anguish.

What resolves: a blurry portrait,
reposing in shattered glass:
A Kandahari mother
missing her wounded husband,
steadies herself on my arm.
I offer a hungry toddler my sanwich.

Turning my back,
suddenly two more tiny girls
peck at it,
three fluttering, hungry pigeons in the park.

My gratitude for being human is boundless,
smeared between two slabs of bread.
My Pashtun sanwich offers a glimpse,
a taste of this precious connection.

THOMAS BECKWITH

A Call to You

Time is undefeated,
but one must not concede to hate.
Each day is a new lease on life,
just like a new chapter in a book.
Now is the time to advocate.
This is more than about protecting
democracy or exposing hypocrisy.

Protest for unity and humanity.
It is about history, which cannot be
rewritten, but it can be repeated.
Resist going back to the past,
or being a refugee of social expectations.

MLK did not dream for nothing.
Obama did use his platform for change,
and hope for nothing.
Diversity, equity, and inclusion,
they're important.

Peace, love, and joy is what
we want to persist.
You have the right to remain silent,
but do you want that to be a part
of your story?

Protest for unity and humanity.
There is no need to sit back and observe
corruption. Resist the temptation of being silent.
Now is the time to be deviant.

Reasonable Doubt

Everybody smiling in his face like they were there,
every step of the way —Did they forget?

Most people gave up on him,
he was written off as another Black boy—
waiting to be enlisted in the system.

His father was a high school dropout.
His mom migrated and didn't get a bachelor's.
Given up on by his own father—

Told he would never live past eighteen.
He fought and defended himself to prove a point.
Left fatherless at thirteen, tracking toward
    a spot in the pen.

Hooping and shooting dice with his boys,
Wasting away on the block and riding dirty.
Grilling the police and failing in school—

Living up to the message in We Real Cool.
Somehow his name was not written
    on the shots fired,
his life was spared to acquire
    the aroma of a diploma.

He was abandoned by his blood with the exception,
of his mom. Uplifted and empowered
      by the unexpected—
A modern-day hero, a man of faith, the dad he
needed, a mere fate.

He was doubted by the masses and trapped
      by the past—
No longer living in fury Now he can see the future,
which is not so blurry.

arlene s. bice

It's Snowing

it shows a beautiful, pure world
one that we can reach out, touch
hold in our palm, until it melts away
to reveal the underside, the grime

snow brings out the internal magic
lovely thoughts that keep generating
deep within, it feeds a blaze of fire
warms our hearts, while our skin cools

build a snow sculpture, dissolve despair
playful youth returns, if only momentarily
but it reveals a brilliant world where hope
refuses to die but grows and spreads joy.

Out of the Cracks

those days of long ago are not forgotten
tucked into my folder of memories
perseverance only, got me through them
where was my hope; I knew of none

a miracle of light shined through, that life
came to an end, eventually hope squeezed
out of the cracks, shined a pathway to follow
cracks are happening now, light bursting forth

out of the darkness come brave men and women
with a will to fight the evil, defend the innocent
the down-trodden with hope and resilience
with knowledge and justice and true morality

like real superheroes, those that can, are
not hidden in masks and colorful costumes
nor are they figments of fantasy imagination
that flow from talented pens and inks of gold

behold! hang on! the cavalry is on the way!
justice will prevail again; we will hold heads
high in the face of the world with pride
our constitution will be more than history.

Down with the Bullies!

bullies are not to be tolerated
be they in school, in the workplace
or in a government that was developed,
imperfectly, but intended, for one and for all

our country, struggling to make life attainable
for each individual, has stumbled, but not fallen
we carry love and gratitude for accomplishments
of the past that we will achieve justice again, for all

hail to thee, brave citizens who have the
qualifications
to avow our lost rights,
    who have the courage to stand up
to the bullies; you fight for those of us
    who have not your
strength; our hearts are full of gratefulness
    for each one!

the modern-day true leaders of democracy list
    grow longer
you will become stronger;
    your names will carry in history
those whose steps you walk in;
    Adams, Chase, Franklin
Hancock, Hopkinson, Jefferson, Stockton;
    need I go on?

SUSI BOCKS

All The Best to You

good lives don't magically appear
although sometimes we wish they just would
fulfilling dreams and desires
the stuff of good lives
also doesn't manifest just because we want them to
there's a formula
yet still not a guarantee
you'll need a few of these things or all...

the force of your passion
the fuel to making things happen
roadblocks that aren't in your way
in addition, luck in some circumstances
knowing the right people
getting the appropriate advice and guidance
a smile during the difficult times
and showing courage while continuing to persevere

may you achieve all that you hope for
and inspire others to achieve their dreams too

It Took a Village

she had a rough start
encountered so many harsh moments
she didn't deserve

but thankfully, life sent her mentors
those who taught her their secrets
those she could lean on when necessary

the lessons she learned gave her stability
offered her more than just a leg up
she had hope for a better future

Are We Capable

throughout history, human beings have been tested
their sanity as well
people have suffered through wars and violence
every imaginable kind
we've been ignorant, disgusting, barbaric and foul
humans
the slaughter of so many innocents has occurred
over and over again
years of repeated bloodshed
and yet, we continue to weigh down this planet with
more destruction
adding more skeletons in the layers of dirt that
surrounds our planet
giving future generations the evidence of our cruelty
it's certainly nothing to be proud of

where is the hope this cycle of insanity will cease
when will the people decide enough is enough
what will become of the earth eventually
how will goodness defeat evil

it all sounds and feels so hopeless
giving into the thinking we're only monsters
makes us forget that it hasn't been all bad
there are those who have brightened lives

changed things for the better
made us feel that life was worth enduring
and showed us how we could have good lives
we are capable of rising up
learning the importance of community
and most importantly, if we know how to love
it changes everything

YASMIN S BROWN

Dual

I am a rocky mountain on your path to victory,
only when you believe in yourself
    can you conquer me.

I am the screams in white noise
    tapping into your insecurities,
with downward spirals as you mentally unravel,
every thought of inadequacy...
    questioning who you
    could be,
for I know the thoughts you have,
fighting against the unbelief.

I am the boulder you try to dodge,
the pebbles you step on without shoes,
    pain when you are crying,
and overwhelming stress
    that keeps your purpose unfulfilled.

I am FEAR!
You are not bigger than me.
at least that is what I tell myself
    when there is no one around,

but my consciousness, and buzzing sound,
followed by the whisper of my conscience,
you know right from wrong...
    now stop the siren dirge,
with your adequacy and bravery,
    you can do anything,

if you just believe in me,
    and who you are called to be,
as light in the darkness, sparkling to draw you close.

I am the smile when you are happy,
    joy without explanation,
one foot in front of the other
    when you feel you cannot make it.

I am FAITH!
in you and all that I am calling you to do,
with prayer and guidance, you got this one day at a
    time,

I am the soles of your feet,
when you step on every pebble
    with divine intervention for every boulder,
and never forget,
I am the rope waiting for you to grab
    when I tap your shoulder.

STEPHEN W. BUCHANAN

Sensational

Beauty can be
found anywhere
Some disagree
But it is there
for you to find
if you're inclined
and choose to do

Making It Worth It

You've got this life
so, make it yours!
Push through the strife!
Ignore the boors!
Use all the joy
you can employ
and be gutsy!

School of Hard Knocks

What's done is done.
It's harsh, but true.
Awful or fun
you can't undo.
Take what was best,
learn from the rest,
and move on through.

JONI KAREN CAGGIANO

A Poet Whole

Whispers in a tormented heart can see
silent anguish that need not exist or breathe to be.
Can love not unburden a banal, cast-iron soul?
As swords and words are forged,
    you can unbar a poet whole.

Don't confiscate your love, for I now fade.
My vessel is twisted and rough, like a painful braid.
Knead my soul and body into dough that will rise;
speak only vital truths
    toward the hail of orange-red skies.

Age covers a body overcome by castigation,
yet even in frost,
    flowers find glory in raw inspiration.
Untwist my tainted armor
    from my weary, broken breast;
let me bake with stamina,
    rise in merit and seize a koala's rest.

Tomorrow

wash away the guns, a black canvas, like buried sin
trails of sorrow, mold on barren graveyard vases
love you - love you not's that should have been
bullies' lost horns;
    shadow regret seeks humane causes

love was lost, under a hand wrinkled,
    like worn pages in a book
lost in a closed, tainted library
    till a sad adult child decided to look

trees spring where I kiss the earth, gifting clean air
built humble clay cabins, and scars
    taught us to share
nursing homes plucked out, like poisons long astray
elderly dance, smell clean beaches,
    watch their grands play

love was lost, under a hand wrinkled,
    like worn pages in a book
lost in a closed, tainted library
    till a sad adult child decided to look
islands of trash ...
    their zip code no longer ... to be
countries of volunteers flew in
    to help clean up the sea
compost tea fertilizer, rain to water,
    bees for pollination
animal lives were treated with respect, appreciation

thanks to a winkled professor
    who found the missing pages
our world came together
    with love in meaningful stages

starlings wept, sensing humans
    could not fail this final test
no living thing unappreciated,
    not even an old bird's nest
billionaires ceased to be,
    for all people eat and have an abode
even fairies provide mushroom circles
    for every homeless toad

Ameliorate

The wind breathes life into our earthly existence.
Time slows around a newborn's brisk arrival.
Pieces of love cling to a lost balloon. Cypress yearns
for the piano player's new melody as they serenely
await.

She holds his serenity like smiling pearls.
Forgiveness is like a leaf well-veined, for love
morphs as it is fed into the tremble of a wing, not
the thunder of a storm. Age brings mercy, for she
inserts herself like monarch parchment where squid
ink seals his name in diary red upon her heart.

Our souls no longer flutter in anguish as humans
wound and inflict cruelty where scars once turned
scarlet. Years of monstrous loss tread weary, and
couples crave longevity, the dance of desire
unremitting. Love said no to entangled threads of
color, sex, size, and beauty being inhaled like an
entrée; life taught us to savor the seamless meal.

Laughter leaves hints of the sun in our air—scents of
a lavender waltz in her thinning hair. He holds her
rounded belly in his hands and caresses the folds of
her face. He muses on their youth and retraces his
memory with clear emerald eyes. Nothing matters
except she is here, no need for whys.

VANESSA CARAVEO

It Comes in Waves

It comes in waves.
First a smile, a tiny ripple,
then a hand, a strong current,
raised in protest of mistreatment,
raised to sit upon a shoulder,
raised to lift a patient up.

Many tormented by waves of pain
due to illness and disease
unable to get necessary treatment
or medicines they need
because of the greedy one percent
who place money over lives.

Waves of Americans eradicated
due to expensive healthcare.
The majority is now waking up
that something must be done.
We must unite and raise our voices.
Injustices toward our health
will no longer be tolerated
so there can be hope for the ill.

First an idea, a small splash,
then policies, tidal waves,
forbidding barriers to entry,
forbidding outrageous prices,
forbidding malicious designs.

Healthcare can get better now
but not in one fell swoop
and not without those tiny ripples
because it comes in waves.

Man Versus Guns

Not us against each other
but instead, Man against guns
and the guns are winning.

Fathers study on a weekday.
A poorly secured cabinet.
A disgruntled teenager.
An opaque backpack.
And the guns win.

A rooftop near the podium.
A controversial politician.
A down on his luck civilian.
A slow-moving target.
And the guns win.

An easy purchase; an easy exam;
an easy to obtain license;
a few loud neighbors and dark thoughts.
Hearts stop beating
when the guns win.

Gun violence must stop
and safer gun laws must be passed
for terror from mass shootings
and a country living in fear
desperately needs change now.

There is still hope man will finally awake
and win the war against gun violence
so we may live in a country
where safety and peace are prioritized
and its citizens are no longer prey.

An Inclusive World

No one can say they're perfect
nor control the way they're born,
so why is there so much prejudice
for the disabled who aren't the norm?

Immigrants who come from afar
are deported to reduce the flow,
but the highly skilled are given jobs
and used so the country can grow.

LGBT people are called sinners
and condemned for who they love,
but the only one who has the right to judge
is our Lord from up above.

The elderly lose their job
and are often pushed aside,
but don't we realize we'll too grow old
and wisdom is something to take pride.

The wealthy look with disdain
at the impoverished for how they live,
but their money would make a great difference
if they donated it and learned to give.

My hope remains to live in a world
where inclusion is found galore
for there is beauty in our differences
when we finally see love and acceptance soar.

THERESA CARLIE

Dirty Work

Headfirst, we plunge into dawn's ashy smear
Feral zealots, embracing the New Year
Gripping glasses like talismans
A sparkling ward against last year's demons

But we awake in the same mess we left
Only just the day before
When we donned our Sunday best
And sidled out the door

Thin breaths rasping in parched throats
Nostrils itching from stale smoke
Eyelids crusted over, yet peering
Finding far away and dim, a germ of hope

So armed with machetes, twine,
Bread crumbs, soft words, wine
Clenched teeth, scissors, a scalpel
Anything we can find

We lurch around each calendar page,
Slipping, sticking, doggedly snipping
The withered brambles that catch our ankles
And send us tripping, sprawling, tangled

Face first into the undergrowth
Where down there in the dirt we see up close
The fragile sprouts, the tiny gains
A future to reap, from our laboring pains

CASSA BASSA

Hope Is in The Air

Friendly smiles
I saw, on the sidewalk
full of hope and optimism

The inflation is high
Our children are obese
We don't feel safe to be out alone at night

But the instant coffee tastes better this morning
Stacked on the kitchen table,
the pile of unpaid bills
looks less burdensome
One egg on toast, instead of two
it solves the egg short supply crisis
and the expanding middle-aged waistline

The wind brushes on our skin
such evidence of things unseen

Even we are still in debt
in poor health and job scarcity
tomorrow is full of possibilities.

Ginger

The stray ginger cat arrives for its daily meal
Full-bellied, it stretches in the afternoon sun
He brushes its coat with an old toothbrush
bristles worn and splayed
"Stay, Ginger!
Here's a home to share."

He sits in his late wife's rocking chair
gazing out at the street
a hustle-bustle world he once knew well
Sipping tea, nibbling a chop-chop cookie
he smiles
planning a trip to the shop for fresh meat
a treat for Ginger

It's something to anticipate each day
a reason to walk
to greet the neighbours
to feel needed once more
to reclaim a sense of purpose and worth
He'll stretch that journey as far as he can
for Ginger.

Window of The World

A grape on the vine
thriving
the sun tiptoes around her smile
The hospital window frames this image

Next to it
it's the vision board
faces of dedicated professionals
snapshots of me in rehab's grip
circling a bold declaration,
"I will walk again!"

Eighteen months
I've called this place home
the Brain Injury Unit
a holiday I never craved.
Dreams of world travel
Scottish castles rising from mist
the Tower of Babel piercing the sky
an African safari's wild heartbeat
shattered
faded

Then you step through the door
a sunflower smile ablaze
offering a kaleidoscope of travel
VR goggles
portals to the world.

I soar above Fuji's sacred peak
tread the Amazon's tangled veins
sway on a camel's back through Sahara
rest by Dunnottar's rugged cliffs
I walk, I skip, I run
laughter spills from my lips

Hope unfurls as wings,
lifting me beyond frail bounds
settling on a reservoir of dreams
a wellspring of what could be.

CARLA M. CHERRY

Hope, Like the Phoenix

A meteor headed for Earth in 2032.
I said, Oh well,
I gave it a good run,
and with all the *good people* who voted for this
administration
racing to turn the clock back 200 years,
let it come, crash at 38,000 miles per hour,
trigger tsunamis to wipe us all away,
wash away venoms that refuse to die–
greed, imperialism, racism, sexism, classism,
heterosexism–
if I get to sit with my family one last time.
My son.
My niece.
My God.
They will not even be 40.
Even then, so much of the world I still will not have
seen.
All the fauna and flora that would die.
What have they done to deserve annihilation?
I scroll for updates about 2024 YR4.
Chance of it entering Earth's atmosphere, almost nil.
And more good news in my feeds–
angry voters screaming about these lies and
betrayals at town halls.
Sit-ins.

People disseminating petitions and lists of anti-DEI
corporations to boycott.
I pass them on.
Newsletters run by activists with call scripts to
facilitate
my daily calls to Senators and Congressman.
Righteous politicians like Bernie.
AOC.
Jasmine Crockett.
Ayanna Pressley.
Maxine Waters.
Tim Walz.
Teachers like me whose bulletin boards and walls are
covered by blackout poems,
quotation shares inspired by banned books and Black
history,
whose student essays are full of empathy for
oppressed characters,
and celebrate the perseverance of their ancestors.

Self-Care Is Resistance

A neighbor texted me about her weekly food
giveaway.
Come grab a bag of produce.

We hug as I thank her.
Come on, take another one. There's plenty!

Organic bell peppers.
Beefsteak tomatoes.
Avocados.

These tomatoes almost sing as I slice them.
I cradle each bell pepper in my hand before I run
them under the faucet.
So crisp under my knife.
Of rich soil, bathed in fresh rain.

These ripened avocados.
Skin easily acquiesces after the first slice of my
paring knife.
I peel the rest away with my fingers.

Vibrant green, thick pulp easily mashed,
blends well with the cubed tomato.
Guacamole atop tacos.

The next night, the green beans.
Mom and I sift through the pile.
Rinse them.
Snap off the ends, snap each bean in half.

I mince garlic,
Slice onions and red bell peppers.
Light boil, then simmer in Bragg's aminos,
sprinkling of cayenne, thyme, and oregano.

We bow our heads, hold hands,
thank the farmers, those who share, and God
for the nectar of human kindness.

LORALEE CLARK

When Capitalism Says

i.
When capitalism says "more"
they mean: let credit cards, bills
    fall through your fingers
into their laps; a promise of exchange for feeling
    better, more desirable
while clothing, cars, new updates amass behind you.

I say, Fine: more.
More real work.
No metaphorical sleeves-push your cotton ones
up to your elbows, sun rising in your throat.
Construct more wildlife bridges over roadways
to decrease deer, raccoon, possum guts
spilled slick on the tarmac or simply
tear up more roadways; they're in the middle
of animals' habitats anyway. Plant over more
lawns with native species: phlox, black-eyed Susan's,
goldenrod. Vervain and Bergamot. Attract more
native bees. Cordon off more areas for communal
gardens. Eat more local veg.
    Grow more herbs to heal
our wounded bodies and minds, dented and battered
more and more.

"More?" Yes: more than a living wage
for bus drivers taking us safely home,
weaving through intersections of
exhaustion and grief of what could be but isn't yet;
for janitors and other cleaners scrubbing our messes;
for teachers shaping our children's futures;
for fruit and veg harvesters making our lives literally
livable, shelves stocked, pantries secure.
More public transport, bike routes and networks.
More multi-generational housing
to combat isolation.

ii.
When capitalism says "not enough"
they mean: to feel happy and whole
you need to squeeze your life-force
shining with possibilities into your job,
sacrifice sanity, family time, sleep.

"Not enough?" I say, right!
Not enough advocation:
let's prepare to deal with the waves
of oncoming diseases so
family members and friends do not accumulate
in hospitals and morgues again.
Not enough pollution control to decrease
smog, toxins, wildfires, floods.

Not enough restorative justice practices:
give stolen land back to its original stewards
that it may regain equilibrium and flourish again.
Not enough gun control to prevent children
fearing death, facing death, through a curriculum
of school shootings. Not enough
wind and solar energies that do less harm
to the earth and her inhabitants.

"Not enough?" Never enough:
Embrace our rageful anger,
mouths twisted, necks red and bellowing;
not enough making peace with our guilt and shame
to motivate changes.
    We still are unable to eat money;
instead extend ourselves to build relationships,
build trust, focus on communal goals.

iii.
When capitalism says "buy"
they mean buy what they are selling:
fear, scarcity, plastics and fast fashion.

I say Yes: buy! Buy into the notion
that enough exists: we have enough resources
to house, feed and care for everyone on this planet.
It is only our economy and its poisoning mindset
    that hoards resources.

How many properties are abandoned, unused?
How much food
is thrown away at the end of a regular business day?
Rather than shared, given, without a thought
    to coin or bill?

Buy into the practice of mutual aid—
what I have, you need. What I may need
you may give. Buy into beliefs that support equity,
community. Wholeness and dignity.

Procure more public spaces
    where communal gathering,
without having to spend, exist. Where free
mental health services are available.
Invest and acquire a sense of place
a sense of belonging that celebrates
humanity, possibility,
depth and honoring.

At nightfall, when we roll down our sleeves,
may we throw back capitalism's rhetoric
of "more," "not enough," and "buy"
at its boated, greasy face.
Reinvent the world we see
into the world that can be.

Traveler's Advice

If you are bound again
run your eyes over the twisted cording
    holding you tight;
curve your wrist. Allow your fingertips
to skim the rough hills and valleys of those fibers.
Don't strain against them.
Instead, understand all the work expended
    to create them:
laying the bark or hair or hide
    with blocks and paddles,
the slivers twisted into hanks
the hanks twisted again, 45-degree angles.
Notice all the tensile strength, braided, binding.
Now breathe.
Let your thoughts circle like a hawk
as the ropes work their magic, affording you
time for clarity of insight.
Taste your wings, their striated feathers
    linked together;
thrust your tongue atop their alignment.
Savor their saltiness in the moment
    before movement occurs
energy coiled and quivering.

Carry your visions upwards into the air,
fruition as you become the hawk, circling above and
bringing yourself back into your bound body.
Remember, discomfort is an illusion; you fit
beyond this arduous space. These ropes are a mirror.
Look into the mirror to see who you are
    beyond this moment.

LAUREN M. CLEMMONS

Democracy Ablaze: A River of 65,000 Voters

My Vote is like a river.
Nourishing the land through which it flows.
Sustaining life. Providing life.

You challenge my Vote.
To disenfranchise me.

You pollute me.
With Industrial byproducts that choke me.
Sewage that dirties me.
Oil and grease that smother me.
Toxic metals that sicken me.
Sediment and erosion that degrade me.
Pesticides and herbicides that weaken me.
Life in my thick, murky waters struggles to survive.

You think you can intimidate me,
      discourage me and alter my flow.
You think you can Kill my Vote.

But the oily, greasy debris that smothers me
      has caught fire.
I am on fire!
I am Enraged!

I am the Mighty river.
I refuse to ooze rather than flow.
The life within me shall not decay.

I am not alone.
Trees of life root my banks.
Tributaries still feed me.
Rain quenches my thirst.
Sun beams upon me.
I hear freedom in the wings flying over me.
I see hope in the eyes that look upon me.

I will flow again!
Nourishing the land through which I flow.
Sustaining life. Providing for the future.

You will Not pollute me.
You will Not disenfranchise me.
My Vote is my voice.
I refuse to be silenced.

I am not alone.
65,000 other Voters breathe and speak with me.
You challenge the lives of 65,000 Votes.
To disenfranchise us.
You think you can Kill 65,000 of us.

But We are the Mighty river.
No longer on fire with rage,
We have been Restored.
We are Maintained by the Rule of Law,
Life flows again in our waters.

You will Not pollute us.
You will Not disenfranchise us.
The Law nourishes us.
Our Votes shall flow like the river
Carrying our elected ones to Victory.*

*Historical references: In 1969 the polluted Cuyahoga River caught fire. This fire served as a wake-up call, leading to the creation of the EPA in 1970, the passage of the Clean Water Act in 1972, and the River's subsequent restoration. In 2024, a NC judicial candidate, trailing by over 700 votes after a recount, challenged the validity of 65,000 votes for his opponent on a technicality.

CANDICE LOUISA DAQUIN

For the day, we are ready

*I want to unfold. I don't want to stay folded
anywhere, because where I am folded, there I am a
lie*

—Rainer Maria Rilke.

It is holy—the room filled with flowers;
    a perfume unable to
synthesize because it is an experience,
    as touching you will
not be translatable—the covet of moments,
    secret and unable
to describe, we fill our silence with breathing,
    until even a slight
rise in temperature can be found.
    A pearl holding the sea in her
center, you asked me, *why the sea?*
    Why not mountains? Forests? Desert.
I wonder what within us, chooses?
    And by what measure
this decision is reached?
    At times I hunger for the dismal fall of perpetual
rain—as familiar as my face.
    Then parched roll of desert tongue, reaching
into infinitum, solaced
    by nothing but her ignited heart.

A punctuation of color
brushed in afterthought,
   eclipsing of an orange sun, cupping
the entire world in her breast.
   It is holy to imagine a place far
where memories are
   conquered and strangeness lost, where
belonging for once,
   from the moment of waking to last traced
thought in sleep.
   Such a place is already in existence—and I
have been told,
   to find it I must look inside myself; for no
amount of running will get me there.
   When I urge escape
I transfer the bags and boxes of all the years,
   but if I close my eyes
and envision this place,
   I can pare down the walls between
us—and walking cliffs edge, cross over.
   I don't know yet
where it is—but like love, we recognize belonging
and belonging recognizes us—
   a promise of some kind held
in the silver that circles moon—
   keeping it centered in a
black ribboned sky. For the day we are ready.

After listening to Pink Floyd in the afternoon

There's a whole world out there, right outside your window. You'd be a fool to miss it

—Charlotte Eriksson.

Run outside, don't speak of it
don't bring waterproof clothing
just go—start like you mean to go on
drop intention, leave behind means of
communication; run if you're not going to
be heckled for it; run faster if you are,
    even if it feels odd
like being ten again, like running away
    from your stuck ways
like strength. You will know where to go,
    don't over think it.
It's there, waiting, have you forgotten?
    Remind yourself. We
stop remembering when taken up
    with all the insubstantial chores
of survival. We throw out our core
    with old clothes and plants that
died even as you tried so hard
    to keep them going through the long
frost of years you stood in place.

But it's still all there. Don't lose
that wonderment you had as a frowning,
    laughing child, give yourself
a push. Keep pushing.
    Sometimes it might feel like dying. Do it anyway.
Watch but don't be watchful.
    Don't be afraid, just this once, be fearless.
March forward like a dance,
     grin and flail your hands. *Insist*.
Own the street. Smile. Then grin.
    Flap your arms. Look crazed in your takeover.
This is it. This is the beginning
    of today and tomorrow and the day after.
Chase yourself into this feeling you can do it.
Because you can.

PETER DEVONALD

A Beginning

Would we still set out the same way
if we'd known all that was to come?

Would we still have embraced the journey
if we'd known every obstacle and problem?

Hindsight is a twisting knife, a wishful lie,
dragging all the beauty down with it.

Instead, we began with hope ever expediency,
we believed in the power of our dreams
    to set us free.

And though the paths were often
    dark, paths shrouded
in endless dark woods full of dread and darkness,

I wouldn't have it any other way, to voyage unaware,
down the rivers of Styx to the Gardens of Babylon.

We embraced our youth, we lived
    our four leaves clover,
mesmerising northern lights shone bright
    to our future.

Sanctified

She wished she could throw her arms
    around the world,
to make it all better, to heal it all with loving words,
to mend the broken hearts and traumatised dreams,
to make the world kinder, fairer,
    a more honest place
to live, for good people to be rewarded,
    put food on the table,
stop having to work three jobs and still rely
    on food banks,

She looked out on her congregation,
    thinning every day,
the young and the old, the broken and the blessed,
the devastated and hopeful,
    only they seemed to find God.
She remembered when the church was full,
    standing room only,
there was a buzz about the place,
    a wild hope that somehow,
somewhere, things could get better,
    that we were loved.

Now the church is mostly used
    as a warm space for those who can't
afford to heat their homes or boil a kettle,
    a place to get away—
seek sanctuary, like refugees in the late middle ages,
before we played death bingo with them
    on the tides of fate.

Once a perfect synergy between light and dark,
    now darkness wins,
we lost ourselves, we lost God,
    we lost it all in the end.

Not what they want to hear though, is it?
That the cruel cacophony of the modern world
    promises so much
and delivers so little, leaves us clinging
    to the life raft as the floods come?
Hope is a four-letter word
    full of desperation and longing,
the desperate desire to live before we die,
    is that too much to ask?
Is that really too much? To work,
    experience and enjoy it all?

They're still waiting, my congregation.
What words to say that aren't hollow,
    facile, muffled?
Bright light shines through ancient
    stained glass windows illuminates us all;
a child plays with the rainbow light,
    a baby giggles; a woman smiles.
There's either hope in nothing
    or hope in everything, and in this moment,
in this vital moment, there is hope
    in everything. She smiles. And begins.

A Liar Who Always Speaks the Truth

The poet is called upon to raise the tone,
to strive for something greater than herself,
something more mesmerising and beautiful,
something transcendent to our dreams.

The poet is called upon to raise the dead,
shine new vibrant lights on all the living,
sanctify the visions that have long since fallen,
make new hopes where there is only ash.

The poet is called upon to be a custodian,
of all that is brilliant and perfect and bright,
to be the best of us, to push our understanding
of this world to the very ends of the earth,
teetering.

The poet is called upon to elaborate on our dreams,
to show new ways of seeing
    our profound imagination,
new ways of seeing our place in the universe,
to relook at nature, to touch the eternal,
    right here now.

The poet is called upon to be more than the generic,
more than pontificating politicians and their
    endless bile,
more than advertising slogans
    we wade through every day,
dreamed up by people
    who should be writing meaning.

The poet is called upon to be
    more than just word salads,
instead to be searingly honest
    about the worries of the world,
build profound palaces of the imagination
    to inspire, to teach,
to yearn for a better world, held
    so nearly within our grasp.

The poet is called upon to always be completely
    true to herself,
to write what matters most to her,
    to look into the void
and bring back whatever dreams
    are shown her to share,
to be fearless, passionate and articulate,
    to always be you.

AALIYAH EL-AMIN

Compassion Overflowing

Listen—
With closed eyes
And an open heart.
Breathe in kindness,
Breathe out compassion,
Radiate Lovingkindness.
Place it on butterflies' fluttering wings,
sprinkling out fairy dust as they flit around.
Settle in the long-forgotten alley shanties,
    softly echo through remote nursing homes.
Let it drift along tree-lined suburban roads,
    knock on pulled-curtain homes
of ignored housewives,
welcome in the latchkey children
or worse, those without a key at all,
living in the hollow shells of old cars.
Let compassion be the cause of the day.
Let it grow within you,
Let it pour out of you.
Lead with a smile, please, and a thank you.
Let hands cook meals, hold babies,
and hug everybody.

NOLCHA FOX

Comfort

Hope walks through

the graveyard of your inherited diseases

to bring you aspirin and chicken soup.

Getting Out

Hope doesn't get out much anymore.
Late-night TV news is depressing.
She knows that she should exercise.
She binge-eats chips and donuts.

She turns off late-night TV news.
She Zumbas every day.
She stops binge-eating chips and donuts.
She fits into a size 2 dress.

Hope Zumbas every day.
She loses weight with exercise.
She fits into a size 2 dress.
Hope teaches you how to dance in the flowers

BARBARA HARRIS LEONHARD

Bully Pain: A Duplex Poem

*Upon hearing Jericho Brown live during Black
History Month 2025*

The bullies savage my open wounds.
I massage their *souls* on the stone school yard.

Their *souls* reek of rank socks and clotted blood.
I bear my soul to my father, a pastor.

He knows of souls; the pastor of prayers.
He was a victim of childhood trauma, too.

A child traumatized by generations of grief
That nearly smothered him in a winter drift.

Packed in snow, his soul set a searing fire
That freed him from an icy death. Resolve.

Released him from a burial in snow and ice.
His prayers fired hope in that lake-effect storm.

Hope storms fires in prayers, resolving trauma
And salving wounds that bullies openly savage.

(Tanka)

Our trauma mutes screams
under water. Our fears rise,
steams courage. Rages
currents. A fierce flow is hope.
How mighty is that river.

I Am Not Agony: A Puente Poem

Upon reading Amanda Gorman during Black History Month 2025

Despair sits with me.
I am a mite, gulping dust,
helpless creator of itch,
an annoyance to poison.
I am an inconsolable bird
flying into a window reflecting
the enemy within.
Breaking my neck.
Breaking my neck.
I am a hunched-over hag,
searching for lost magic in
the shadow of imminent death.

"The new dawn blooms as we free it. For there is
only light if we are brave enough to see it, if only
we're brave enough to be it." — Amanda Gorman

I dream of the stars,
which gave birth to my lung air,
my cells, my iron-hot blood.
I am a glorious nova.
My outbursts dwarf the darkness.
I will consume it.
I dream of Earth's wet womb.
I am her maker of meadows.
I am her magma, her fire,
ready to rise.
I dream of the great pine, Methuselah.
I too bristle with the ages. Live on air.
Survive.

MARK ANDREW HEATHCOTE

For the betterment of something

Let me unbridle myself entirely.
And break free from these chains and bonds.
Let me lean on my wings and fly westerly.
On a breeze, and let my heart abscond—

And leave the past and find true meaning.
Let me disperse like a fog, a mist
and discover a rainbow still beaming.
Let me fall in love and with my heart enlist.

In all these social galas where I might shine
let the relics of the past burn charcoal
for I am a kaleidoscope, a picture divine.
If I change, I do it for the betterment of something,
not to startle you.

I might marionette-like a fine red wine.
Take on social responsibilities and more civic duties.
Like I mean to be someone and be less byzantine
Cut through the bureaucracy of these awful
congruities.

I might save the planet or even help somebody.
I might become more public-spirited.
And be the voice of hope instead of perfunctory
And ring the changes no matter how difficult.

Working to ring another's liberty bell

As individuals under one banner
We arrive for work, striving in our roles.
To support fellow citizens and members
To live rewarding lives and meet their goals.

As part of a personalised-centred
Approach; we clarify what is working well.
Note their hopes, their dreams. This is entered
For group discussion, it rings a liberty bell.

And helps us to build up a personal profile.
What is it we admire? How best as a team?
Can we go about our roles and go that extra mile?
Makes a difference, and ultimately, all succeed?

Here everyone we support is unique.
Each is valued and helped to achieve
Ultimately, this is what we all believe.
And hand in hand, socially we help to interweave.

DUANE L HERRMANN

In Troubling Times

We must reach out
to other hearts:
we must! We must!
For only
in such communion
will we find strength
and courage
to continue on—
while the world around
descends to madness.
We are not alone
as it may seem.
And others too
need our courage
and companion
to carry on—
and we shall,
day by day.

Specks of Purpose

Writers on the prairie
gather together
from wide reaches
of grass and grass and grass.
Wind blows
ideas, thoughts, imagination,
limitless as sky
surrounding
every human speck
tiny in the wind.
Contrast creates
dichotomy, contemplation,
originality and words
in strings of being.
As they write
volumes emerge
and civilization
steps forward.

Do Not Admit

I did not want,
did not desire,
to admit this, but...
pain is helpful,
even necessary
for growth, expansion,
and development
of the soul and mind,
and even, body.
Pain tells a limit,
a barrier marking
what was before,
and now comes after.
Soil that is not plowed
does not bear much fruit.
A tree not pruned,
gives poor fruit.
Plowing and pruning
cause pain first,
then benefit.
Welcome pain
into your life
knowing
that growth will come.
It is this hope
that carries me on
to the Glorious end!

TINA HUDAK

Playground of Possibilities

My country's fear is
gripped by NO. These
two are best of friends.
Fear of the other.
Fear of one another.
YES lays sleeping,
grown weary of daily,
often hourly,
struggles.

Hope lies with MAYBE.
Teeter-totters of possibilities.
Green grass sprouts under
foot with sometimes, YES.
Other times, NO.
Hope grows on one
side and equally,
the other.

Good Intentions

To do good in the world is what
I planned. To own a funky
apartment in New York City with
busy streets. To strut those city
sidewalks below while wearing
fashionable clothing even into old
age. To be a savvy lawyer getting it
right, for those who could not.
Finding justice in some dark
corner and throwing it out
into the sunlight.

Life intended otherwise. Raising
sons, filling the house with
boisterous voices of family
and friends. Loving a husband,
always, who is hard to love.

Holding a pen and drawing letters
in ink. Scolding young school
boys with soft sounds and affection.
Befriending birds and green things.
Writing these words.

MICHAEL INGRAM

Black Atlas Shrugged

They had made him a world and forced him to carry it on his back. They thought it would break him, silence him, and weaken him. Because he'd been colonized not to question, bastardized to destroy family bonds and kindred affections, and subsidized to ensure that he did not make the connection.

Black Atlas shrugged.

They had made him a world and forced him to carry it on his back. A world where marginalization and fear permeated the air—stifling his creativity—suffocating his sense humanity. Channeling his energies in directions that exhausted his resistance and made him deny the majesty of his ancestral existence.

Black Atlas shrugged again.

They had made him a world and forced him to carry it on his back. A world that created co-dependence and made him feel as if he could not live without assistance.

Black Atlas shrugged again.

They had made him a world and forced him to carry it on his back. Yet, like a coat that does not fit, one day he lifted it off his back and held it above his head—for their world was not big enough to contain his mind—was not strong enough to break his back—was not proud enough to possess his spirit. And like a toy tossed unconcernedly from a small child's hands, he dropped their world to the ground beneath his feet. The earth trembled with possibility. The air crackled with newfound freedom. And, from the debris that reeked of indignity and false superiority, he reached down and created his own world. A world made from the richly sweet-smelling clay

found on the shores of West Africa and in the depths of the Atlantic Ocean—dark clay that told the story of separation from the motherland, the Middle Passage, and the sands of a foreign land.

Yes, he'd made his own world. Fashioned from the soul of Martin Luther King's dream, the haunting songs of Billie Holiday's truth and the revolutionary style of Langston Hughes' verse. A world that embraces his color and gives him the strength and resilience to uplift both his sister and his brother. Black Atlas shrugged no longer. For he'd made his own world, and he lifted it above his head, and he said, "See God! It is as you said it would be."

Beneath the Shade of the Sheltering Tree

Once, beneath the shade of the sheltering tree— near the clear, cool waters of the river called America— A man sought refuge from the blistering heat of the oppressive and callous sun. He was thirsty for the clear, cool water. He yearned to taste its elusive goodness, goodness so sweet that it promised hope of a brighter and better day. Yet, he was afraid to drink. He'd heard the story that if he placed his colored hands into the river called America, he would contaminate it, and it would never taste as good. So, beneath the shade of the sheltering tree— near the river called America, he sat and clasped his colored hands and cried. Oh, how he cried.

After a while, a penniless child joined him. She, too, sought refuge from the battering heat of the brutal sun. She had lived an impoverished life. Yet, like the man before her, she was afraid to drink. She had heard the story that if she placed her impoverished hands into the river called America— she would dirty it, and it would never taste as good. So, beneath the shade of the sheltering tree— near the river called America, she sat and clasped her unwanted hands and cried. Oh, how she cried.

Before long, a man with disabilities sought refuge from the unrelenting heat of the indifferent sun. He'd lived a shunned life, befriended only by resolve and determination. Yet, like them, he was afraid to drink. He had heard the story that if he placed his shunned hands into the river called America, he would change it, and it would never taste as good. So, beneath the sheltering tree— near the river called America, he sat and clasped his unwanted hands and cried. Oh, how he cried.

As time wore on, a recently immigrated family joined them. They had moved from distant lands seeking refuge from the burning sun. Yet, like all of them, they were afraid to drink. They had heard the story that if they placed their alien hands into the river called America— they would infect it, and it would never taste as good. So, beneath the sheltering tree— near the river called America, they sat and clasped their unwanted hands and cried. Oh, how they cried.

Finally, beneath the shade of the sheltering tree near the river called America, all of them desiccated from life and wasted tears. Their thirst grew— so grew their collective strength to risk it all and drink what was so close yet seemed so far. So, they all cupped their disgraceful, shunned, alien hands and dipped them into the river called America, and they drank. It tasted good! It tasted sweet! They realized that their hands did not pollute the river. It only knew the nature of their hearts, souls, and minds.

Their drinking from the river called America didn't spoil it or stain it. All of their hands helped to replenish it, and they drank to finally receive strength, and they drank following wherever the river went. How they drank! Partakers of the clear, cool waters of the river called America!

My Mother and My Father

My mother never loved my father. My father never loved my mother. Their relationship was abusive from the start. Entered against her will. He was forceful. Taking, robbing, raping. Her spirit faded into ghostly shadows, ghastly and fearful, and she was so achingly alone. She had no friends anymore, nor family or place to call her home; her dignity was a dry dungeon abandoned, to which he told her she would never return. His violence was an ocean's ebb and flow, an endless source. Unpredictable, slow, quick, and mocking; he called her ugly in front of his friends. They laughed and called her ugly too. He was a master of humiliation, and she did not know what to do. His lust was unmanageable, with raging jealousy and possessiveness. He knew of her hatred and how his touch was despised.

Cold
fingers.

Cold   manhood.

At night in the darkness, he rejoiced whenever she cried or pleaded, "Please, no more perversion." His insatiable appetite to assault her extended to his friends. Friends who used her to no end– "Please stop, I can't take it, please, I'm dying."

He said, "Pity for you, victim? We have none. And we will defile you beyond the rising sun. You could have walked through an open door, but the way is shut, and now you must stay tough." So, he was vigilant, watching, gauging, and guessing. Would she try to escape, seeking mercy north of his grip? He was a man scarred and uglier with each passing sin. And there was no way to remember all of them.

Yet, despite it all, she was still majestic, born of noble character and determination. The ability she had to nurture us to be courageous children, now, as men and women, despite our violent roots, we know somewhat of the truth.

I am a child of an abusive relationship:
My mother's name is Africa.
My father's name is America.

CHYREL J. JACKSON

Recorders of Truths Onyx Light

For such a time as this the
Black writer must
Persist.
With a rigid insistence
and dogged persistence
we must chronicle our
Narratives, poems, and write
our words.
Making our voices heard.
Releasing them into the
Universe.
Let them settle in the
atmosphere as summer
rains that cover the earth.
In the face of:
Literature bans,
Culture erasure,
Whitewashing of
Black History,
and the seizure of
Black speech.
The Black writers must
PERSIST.
RESIST, RESIST, RESIST.
Now's our time to Stand up.
WOKE is awareness.
Awake we must remain.
Watching in vigilance.
Protecting Black personhood
with all our due diligence.
We don't shrink.

We don't take down.
We record the facts.
This is our time to
stand tall and Rise.
Let us meet this
moment with hope.
Let our words resonate
truths Onyx light.
Look at us Shine.
We sparkle and we Shine.

Satchmo's Melody

The indelible resilience of
the human spirit can't be
put into words.
We cry, we hurt, we fall
apart.
Most days through times
of sorrow it's difficult to
breathe.
Some of us lose so much
We weep and grieve.
The very next day, we look
up to a bright sunny sky
in that very moment our
spirit revives.
We see the colorful
rainbow of our lives.
With new inspired eyes and
drive.
We live we thrive.
We create purpose during
life affliction.
We rise, we sing, we write,
recounting the stories and
meaning of our lives.
Finally we dance and center
our hurt.
Rejoice, finding self-worth.
The soul magically over time
heals itself.

We carry the spirit of the elders
and Ancestors deep within our
hearts.
In one voice within that moment
of healing we sing out in joy
Satchmo's melody:
And I think to myself what a
what a wonderful world.

Hope is on the Horizon

Life is filled with pain and sadness.
When your season of grief is over,
the sun comes up, but through all
that is experienced always
Look up.
For every rejection,
no,
loss, and
redirection.
We start over again hopeful,
somewhere within us lies a new
perspective.
We foster new direction.
Look up.
Holding our heads to the sky.
Defeat is not an option, purpose
is only revealed the moment we
hurdle past sorrow and pain.
The moment that we are willing to
try.
Success is never born absent of
failure.
Continue the path letting go of all
negative and stagnant behavior.
Look up just beyond the horizon.
Every new day unseen miracles are
possible.

Unseen miracles are possible.
Hope can move mountains.
Faith can move mountains
You can achieve great things.
Don't be afraid to go after your
dreams.
The strange fruit heritage we are
wondrous beings.
Most wondrous beings.

ZANETA V. JOHNS

Keep Going

We are mustard seeds in this colossal universe
We are champions of hope
We are a communal forest—trees
        anchored deep within the earth
We stand upright and determined
Our presence requires us to act—
        to imagine infinite possibilities
        to reach toward the heavens
        to change the status quo
        to advocate for justice
        to speak out
        to be better

Never give up
Lock arms and hearts
Use tension as fuel
Eyes fixed ahead, declare triumph
Every step forward is progress—
        from the first daring step
        to the gallant march
        to the valiant leap
We are entrenched and ever-blooming
Keep hoping
        Keep loving
                Keep going!

Future Leaders

Housing projects and trailer parks are
          full of future leaders
Children whose dire circumstances
          may slow them down
          but nothing will hold them back

Some children are destined for greatness
Look beyond their circumstances
          to imagine their potential
Ponder beyond your assumptions
          to envision future leaders

They eat red gravy ... biscuits and bacon
At times, cereal without milk
They wear hand-me-down clothes
          too-tight shoes and secondhand jackets

Look closely into their somber eyes
          of varied shapes and colors
You'll see them again decades from now
          in the cockpit
          at the front of classrooms
          beside you at conference tables

Admire their precious tiny hands
        in all complexions
You'll see them again holding scalpels
        conducting an orchestra
        painting a masterpiece

Listen intently to their voices—
        shy and noticeably unsure
You'll hear them later forecasting the weather
        commanding order in the courtroom
        accepting a Nobel Prize

Don't judge or underestimate them
Someday you'll seek their wisdom and expertise
Someday, one of these incredible children
        just might become your President!

Frigid Season in the USA

Snowflakes drifted gently over the landscape
I awakened to shock, sadness and sunshine
It is a frigid time in the USA
Division threatens our humanity
As we enter a season of darkness
      we must be the light
We are stronger than the storm—
      always have been
God has a reason for every bleak season
God allows the earth to quake
Though times ahead are frightening
Remember who sparks the lightning

Televise the transformation of our nation
Through monsoon tears we watch
We contest the political mudslide
We refuse to backslide
Truth will ultimately prevail
To those who spew vileness about race
      know that we are covered in grace
We are a mighty people
Our enduring works can't be erased

We've been here before—
We know that spring follows winter
We know that summer follows spring
God sits at the helm—never overwhelmed
      We remain vigilant
      We remain hopeful
It may be frigid in America
      but God is still in control!

LIN MARSHALL BRUMMELS

Advice for the New Year

*People who avoid their own feelings will neglect
yours.*
>   Jennifer Pagliaroli, Bethlehem, Pa.,
>   *New York Times*

Drink good coffee.
Read, read, read, write.
Take time to pet your cat,
listen to the purr.

Care for old people,
dogs, horses, and other critters
in your sphere - you too
are aging and may need help.

Look at the stars on clear
early mornings,
sit in pools of sunshine
shining in south windows.

If you live where there is snow
bend your legs,
not your back to shovel it,
watch out for ice.

If injured get help,
pass up hospitals if you can
but see a doctor
as needed.

Avoid political news,
discussions and arguments.
Disagreements
build fences.

Spend time with people
who love.
If they do not love themselves
they will neglect you.

Chatter

You may get thru the world, but it'll be very slow
if you listen to all that is said as you go...

    —June Brander Gilman, *People Will Talk*

Squirrels chatter to each other daily,
joyfully jump from ash branches
    to blue spruce's stiff bows.

Try not to panic when your computer hiccups
poems and spreadsheets
    are temporarily locked away.

Chat with sheepdog Pickles about your worry,
she never jumps to conclusions,
    listens with one ear tilted.

Talking heads on social media blather on.
Everything you hear concocted by AI bots
    to divide us.

Look to the heavens to clear your head,
survey the clouds for an antidote to day's iota
    of bad news.

Courage to be Vulnerable

Our friend destiny, closes doors,
opens windows, to let in light,
pushes folks out of dark places.
We all feel lost when life
makes a turn we did not ask for.
We must be patient for new visions
to form, learn to let go of dim pasts,
look ahead, picture renewal.
New directions do not come easy.

Sometimes it is an unwanted divorce,
a separation of souls. Advice from
my divorce attorney seemed silly
at first but turned out to be
quite helpful, "Don't hurt him."
This admonition stilled my hand
from scratching his car with
evil epitaphs and banging him
on the head with an iron skillet.
Society demands us to move on,
so, move ahead we must.
Other times an election does not
go as we wish. Some will declare
they must go, leave the country,
but most of us will stay. Politicians
ebb and flow. Look around, find ways
to support causes to believe in,
make a difference, give to causes
like flood or fire relief, open a door

for another, volunteer time
to read to children, drive an elder
for groceries, offer counseling
regardless of ability to pay. Each
offering shines a wee light into dark days.
When a better future is glimpsed,
courage or a symbolic kick
in the pants may be needed
to get us out of the doldrums.
Moving ahead against the tide
requires internal fortitude,
strength and untapped reserves,
often surprising ourselves.
Open our arms to new people.
Allow ideas to incubate,
illuminate the path ahead.

DANIELLE MARTIN

Robes of Hope

A grey waddling mass of fur
pauses at an unfamiliar bend,
where greenage and pitch converge.
Looking beyond the haze of shiny metal
black orbs, pools of jumbled words,
sentences telepathically connect
and we too, awkwardly stop.
As this grey, black waddling mass of fur
gives a quick nod, so pleased, making peasants stop.
Unbothered, lavish lifestyle exposed,
this grey, black waddling mass of intriguing fur
in robes of bright, bold hope,
    lives to see another day.

Humanity Begins Within

There is much that I want, much more than I need
perhaps it's a craving, a greed,
    humans nurse into being
that can never be repelled, as we fall out of self
away from our truth, into an emptiness without end,
a cursed desire for despair, until we begin
    to inch deep into self again,
forgotten seeds, aching to be
    in this ad-hoc world band.
Oh, if we could harmonise, we'd surely heal,
embracing the flux and edging differences that sting,
gobbling up less, while loving more,
making, "Do unto others as you would
    have them do unto you" law.
For when we see self in others, perhaps,
the savage greed that feeds will starve
and a society etched with a persistent memory
    of past wrongs, will value all life forms
giving much more than we need,
    without having to want,
for indeed, humanity begins within.

DAVID MARTIN

Awake

Awake in the night, I hear Charley,
our 9-pound, white Pomeranian
breathing deeply in the moonlight,
rubbing his face on the carpet,
almost crying for help

to remove the crusty, dried "tears"
that form routinely below his eyes.
After warm water applied with a damp
cloth, a secure arm wrapped around his
chest, he allows the problem to be removed,

and although grumpy and wishing he didn't
have to go through this weekly drill, his breathing
pattern changes, and he grows calmer,
    even grateful.
To experience kindness from all creatures
    is a blessing
to the receiver and the giver.

Contact, instead of control,
is the secret to understanding
and living together.

We All Do

"Procrastination is the art
    of keeping up with yesterday," someone said,
so I made a point to be early to my first class
    one semester. When entering
the room, I was confronted by the teacher,
    a tall, bearded man wearing
dark pants, a white, long-sleeved shirt,
    a plain, black tie, and large sunglasses.

He listened to each person walk into the room,
    cross the floor, and
sit down. When the class was full,
    he appeared to see with his ears.
Those glasses signified that his vision
    was impaired, but he showed
us his hearing was acute. He smiled and said,

"The sun rises in the East and sets in the West.
Oh, it's hard to tell which lover will treat you best."
I heard laughter in the back of the room, and
    Mr. Surrido
grinned, again, showing beautiful, white teeth.

Before long, I felt the room change.
  It soon appeared not to
have a ceiling or walls to block us
  from expanding our vision, and
I felt an amazing undertow of ardor
  that was refreshing. That spirit
encouraged me to bloom
  with creativity and "perchance to dream."

Life became full of mysteries:
  Bigfoot, Sasquatch, Jackalope, furbearing
trout, and God, but I did not hear
  our blind teacher call out for evidence and
proof of my thesis. He did not ask for "belief"
  in my research. He smiled, when
I spoke of a country, this promised land of joy,
  grace, and hope.

"In the evenin' when the sun goes down,
it's hard to keep on livin' without a frown."
The students learned to metaphorically
  juggle words and concepts.
He whispered, "TAPS is the most powerful music
  with 24 notes in a row."

Good literature is a collection of
    our culture's intelligence and wisdom.
With names, burden, happiness,
    smiling, and confidence may enter the room.
With three little pigs and one wolf,
    houses get blown down.
"May the season's true gifts be yours."

At the end of one class, Mr. Surrido
    raised his right hand toward the ceiling to quiet
the students. "I had just moved to an address
between Sunrise Avenue and Sunset Blvd,
two streets in San Francisco, and was explaining
to a clerk where my home was located
for billing purposes. 'I live between Sunrise and
Sunset,' I told her."

"Oh, honey," she knowingly replied, "we all do."

SARAH MERRITT RYAN

Light We Feel

Light we see
Inside us yearning
Behind our eyes
Optimism abounds.
Sentiments hold
Truth and connection
Bind us hither
Standing than sitting
Ready to demand
Sense and reason
Compassion utmost
Forging existence.
Two realities clash
Well-meaning both
Reason testing
Reconcile we
Can we?
Sake of children
Act as adults.
Feel us brightness
Warm resolution
Guide us out
This tempest being.

TERRI MICHELS

Civil Rights Beatitudes

Blessed are the peacekeepers
    guided by a moral compass,
for God will shelter them beneath His wings.
Blessed are the marginalized,
    suffering under oppression and injustice,

for they will rejoice in the salvation of God.
Blessed are the hungry and the thirsty,
for they will be nourished at God's banquet.
Blessed are the business owners
    who have lost everything,
for their fortunes will be restored to glorify God.
Blessed are the innocent children,
for they are all equal in the eyes of God.
Blessed are the unheard and unseen,
for God hears their cries and sees their pain.
Blessed are those who persevere in their work,
for they will find comfort and rest.
Blessed are the humble and faithful servants,
the hands and feet of God,
    bringing peace to the streets.
For they will be bathed in His grace and mercy.

KARUNA MISTRY

Compassionfruit

consume the compassionfruit
some refuse to sip its juice
they ignore what seems a chore
often making others feel rotten
compacting society's problem
make a change to rearrange
think and have a sober drink
philanthropy or social atrophy
in haste, don't forget to taste
consume the compassionfruit

CommUnity

nuclear families tend to explode
rather, they domestically implode
if we think we are the centre of our lives
our circle of self unashamedly amplifies
listen, the false ego kills all and thrives!
communal living is easy thinking
easy if you want social easing
keep the nuclear units, the family spirit
keep the marriage vows, let cohabitees be proud
keep privacy private but strengthen public rebate
this is not the communist or socialist debate!
be civil, let children learn to intermingle
let juveniles and new adults be responsible
share breathing spaces, food and resources
joint brother-sisterhood in cosy neighbourhoods
no need for us to bring guns and knives
community crime is solved overnight
our ammunition, to create a safe space
a lasting community for the future

DAVION MOORE

What's Next?

A time of uncertainty
A time of division
Where do we go from here?
What lies ahead of us?
What do we do?
We spread kindness
We help others
We work towards
A better future
We stay upbeat
Rise when we fall
Cry if you need to
Smile after
We lead
We learn
We laugh
We live
We love
With all our hearts
And believe
The days will get better

Hope, Hope, Hope

Hope
Optimism
Positivity
Enthusiasm
Happiness
Outstanding
Peace
Empathy
Helpful
Opportunity
Pleasing
Enjoyment
Harmony
Open
Purity
Equal
Healing
Our
People
Everyday

NIMITOK

Small Chops

Small Chops; Small Talks
Lest they own my experience,
And for a while, hold my attention.
But!
I would find filling in a solid meal,
Count the calories and weigh them real.
Sane is my accent, sometimes unconventional,
Not just a deluded mind but mingling with the
sensational.
I promise that this course is justice,
Closely aligned with chivalry's practice.

Small Chops; Familiar Party
Rice to the rescue of the masses?
While the malady of the Lord prays them extinct.
Why?
A man stood tall, an advantage of his kind,
Spoke another language to free his mind.
Slowly, he lost himself in his mouth,
Bombastic culture—now cast out.
Renewed hope springs from this art,
A transient for creatives set apart.

Small Chops; Small Homes
Our iconic blueprints—unaffordable dreams,
Luxury's chase splits the seams.
Else!
Our lands gleaned, left rustic and bare,
The hand that tills, withered in despair.
The young blood spills, staining the earth,
How did minor specifics eclipse the majority's worth?
The hunter forgets—he too will lie beneath,
Six feet down, a meal for worms to feast.
What global plan will our spirit release?

We Live Today

Blindfolded in the uttermost darkness,
Awareness thick as woven chiffon.
Even shadows learn to vanish,
Shamed by the absence of light.
The thunderous applause to the rain—
Be it gross, be it shower?
Is it cleansing or condemning?

Foiled by the foolishness of our actions,
The waste of our remains returns to dust.
Yet, the light—unyielding—shines.
Grateful, we tread its illuminated path,
Afraid to stray, unsure of its end.
Shout! What shall we shout?
Are we ready? We live today!

But within the blindness, truth hides,
Not in sight, but in soundless whispers.
The echoes of storms, of seeds unsown,
A silent call to the weary traveler.
Do we seek or simply stumble?
The path winds; the lamp flickers.
Is it purpose or merely fate?

We live today! Shout tomorrow waits,
A folded parchment, its ink yet wet.

Creatives In the Wild

Though the tales of yester-years hurts
Today, the blow may hit our pelvic
Tomorrow we will be creatives in the wild.

AMI OFFENBACHER FERRIS

Sea Town

A little sea port town
sitting right on the coast
there's so many sites
I can't help now but boast

The houses are grand
far grander than most
I could never imagine
being one of their hosts

I'd never complain no not at all
my little abode's a gem with ease
My flowers are bright and dance
with my trees in the breeze

I hope you will visit
I hope you will come
see my home and my place
happy 'neath the sun

HOPE

H is for helping others to overcome trials, challenges, disasters, and despair.

O is for overcoming prejudice to offer love and assistance to all, no matter their color or gender or sexual practices.

P is for promising to perform to the best of our abilities within our communities to support and nurture one another.

E is because everyone deserves love. Everyone deserves care. Everyone deserves assistance. Everyone needs HOPE.

Holy Water

Clear holy water
languid and cold
Touched to a babes head
keeps the shadows away

Birds cross through
a silver cloud
a hallowed opening
to spark hope within

The magic of the moment
the tightly woven love
The sweet sound of bird song
rings aloud truth will come again

The babe's eyes open
glistening with love
The pastor returns him
into the arms as their beloved

DAWN PISTURINO

Common Ground

The politics of fear,
The politics of hope.
Political pundits play both sides,
Talking a good game
And telling people what they want to hear.
But people, one to one,
Relate to each other on a different level:
Common ground.
Family, struggles, obstacles, money,
Love, faith, conflict, resolution.
Sharing giggles and tears,
Enjoying a meal together,
Swapping stories and jokes.
The human experience.
Everyone has hopes and fears.
All people struggle to survive.
Black, white, brown – no difference.
Inside, we all bleed red,
From conception to dissolution.
Life is too short to spend it on hate.
Embrace one another in the spirit of love.

POEMSOFCAMA

Time

When your eyes open
I hope you embrace the fullness
of love life laughter
When time pauses and rolls
Again
I hope you drift into realms
beautiful and ephemeral
I hope you reach for depths
wondrous and ecclesiastical
When you view the world
Again
I hope it is the atmosphere
of ecstasies and joys
I hope it is the clouds
of realities and truth
I hope it is the home
of your dream and rest
I hope you fly in galactic galaxies
I hope your laughter touches my soul
And I look forward to walking with you
I hope your hope comes with singing
You know that is all you left me with

LINETTE RABSATT

Freedom

break the bondage of my soul
and make me whole and strong
my mind is too long in captivity
and my destiny is freedom
hurt and ignorance almost swallowed
and deeply hollowed my heart
but I have hope for a future
unsealed without structure and
and away from my wardens
where I can give and nurture others
and help them to unlock their chains
with a goal to sustain their freedom
from the ignorance, snobbery and guises
set to compromise our life's anchor - our freedom

Hope

For some,
it's just another day.
For most,
they'll go along their merry way.
For others,
they take life as it comes.
For most
are glad for the morning sun.
For me,
it's a time for reflection,
because you
have been an inspiration
to me
and to many others,
because you
are always willing to help your brother.
To you,
I hope light shines on your way
because you
show love every day.
With you,
I know God walks by your side.
so you
will always in his love abide.

IVAN SALAZAR

A Future of Possibilities

In the dawn of tomorrow, where visions take flight,
We stand on the threshold, bathed in pure light.
With hearts full of purpose, we gaze toward the sky,
In the tapestry of dreams, our spirits will fly.

Oh, the possibilities beckon, like stars in the night,
Each one is a reminder of the strength in our sight.
With the courage to dream and the will to believe,
We carve out a future where all can achieve.

From the whispers of nature, we learn to be wise,
In the rhythm of seasons, in the dance of the skies.
With the pulse of the earth guiding each step,
We nurture our planet, and in gratitude, we prep.

Oh, the beauty of sharing in this magnificent quest,
We rise as a community united and blessed.
With hands joined together, we'll build and create,
In the spirit of kindness, we'll open each gate.

For we are the dreamers, the keepers of the flame,
In the echoes of history, we honor each name.
In the journey of life, we weave our own fate,
In the echoes of time, we find our place great.

Through the lens of tomorrow, we step into light,
Embracing our stories, our futures in sight.
For a future of possibilities is waiting for us,
In the heartbeat of hope, we place all our trust.

And as we forge onward, with courage in hand,
Let compassion be our guide, our vision so grand.
In the embrace of the world,
    where dreams intertwine,
We celebrate together; our spirits align.

United in purpose, our dreams shining bright,
We strive for a future where every heart takes flight.
In the symphony of life, let our voices resound,
In the tapestry woven, together we're bound.

For in every heartbeat, in each whispered prayer,
Lies the promise of hope, a world we can share.
In the future of possibilities, with courage we stand,
Hand in hand, together, we nurture this land.

Let love be our anchor, let justice our guide,
In the future of possibilities, let our hearts abide.
For in every small act, in each kindness we share,
We build a foundation, a world truly fair.

In this chapter of hope, may our spirits take flight,
With dreams intertwined,
    we'll shine through the night.
For the legacy we foster is a beacon so bright,
In the future of possibilities, we'll rise with delight.

Life

In this alley of existence,
Where shadows play hopscotch with light,
I wander,
A question mark in a world of exclamation points,
Irony drapes my shoulders
Like a tattered shawl,
Curtains fluttering in the wind
Of unspoken thoughts.

Life, you whisper,
Is not a riddle to be solved;
It's a dance on the edge of a roof,
A cigarette stubbed out in the ashtray of the cosmos.
Yet here I stand,
A philosopher without a pipe,
My thoughts scattered like autumn leaves,
Caught in the wind's cruel laughter.

With every sunrise,
The world spins anew,
A canvas splashed with colours,
Each hue a memory, a dream.
What does it mean, this waking dream?
To live is to stumble,
To trip over the roots of yesterday,
To embrace the chaos,
Like a child chasing a kite in the rain.

Is meaning a mirage,
Or a sip of water
From the well of our shared humanity?
We gather in the marketplace of existence,
Haggling with our hopes,

Bartering with our fears,
While the sun, indifferent,
Paints our follies in gold,
The echo of laughter mixing with tears.

Yet still, I chase,
Like a moth to the flame,
The flicker of connection—
A smile, a touch,
The fleeting glance that pierces the veil.
Life, it seems,
Is not a question but a chorus,
A cacophony of voices
Singing in the key of now,
Where every note is a heartbeat,
Every pause, a breath of possibility.

Today let us dance, my friends,
In this imperfect, messy, beautiful life,
For meaning is not found in the quiet of
contemplation,
But in the wild, unkempt joy of living,
Where every stumble is a step,
And every question,
A song waiting to be sung.

This Too Shall Pass

Two centuries, like rivers, winding through,
From horse-drawn carts to skies of gray and blue.
In this grand theater of endless change,
    we've seen the old,
The new, in strange exchange.

Like seasons that take their turn,
Never delay, the world unfolds in its unique way.
From quill and ink, where words once flew,
To digital screens, where thoughts pursue.

War's thunderous roar, and peace's gentle hush,
In life's grand story, it's all part of the rush.
From bustling streets to the woods so still,
We've wandered through landscapes, had our fill.

In every moment, like a butterfly's fleeting wing,
The world transforms, a chameleon of everything.
From steam's caress to silicon's cold grasp,
The world keeps turning in a never-ending clasp.

The pace of life, like a runaway steed,
In this grand parade, we find what we need.
Yet, through the turmoil, through all the toil,
We'll find our footing in this timeless soil.

A simple truth, like a lighthouse's guiding beam,
In every storm, every shadow, and every dream.
The sun will rise, as the darkness fades away,
This too shall pass, and we'll see a brighter day.

Now, take the chance, embrace the world's array,
In our ever-changing play, we'll find our way.
Through trials and tests, through joy, through woe,
This too shall pass, and onward we'll go.

With open hearts, like sails on the open sea,
We'll navigate the waters, wild and free.
For in this world of fleeting dreams
    and endless night,
This too shall pass, as we journey towards the light.

Like the moon that wanes but will always return,
Through lessons we learn and bridges we'll burn.
The ebb and flow, the twists, the bends,
This too shall pass, as one story ends.

Two centuries, a tale of the ages told,
With ink and pixel, and stories both young and old.
In this grand tapestry of hope and despair,
This too shall pass, and we'll breathe the air.

MUNMUN SAMANTA (Sam)

Life after Ruins

Silence weighs here heavier,
the air smells only of ash and chemicals.
Buried beneath the rubble of collapsed dreams,
thousand heartbeats have gone to sleep.
Only walls of hatred and vengeance
stand tall.
Voices of humanity tremble and fall.
Here darkness chokes the sunlight.
It is a land of eternal night.

Each breath is punctuated with bullets and bombs.
Grief is the only shared language ensconced
     inside the tombs.
Children's laughter has ceased to peal.
No one mourns for the unborn.
Unspoken words troll the memories.
It is a land of brutal ceremonies.

In this land of dead
One day rain trespasses,
soaking the gunpowder to dust.
Faint light pierces the dark crust of despair.
The glimmer of hope shimmers
     on the eastern horizon.
Pushing through the broken bones
     of concrete sprout two green leaves.

The world welcomes their audacious footfalls.
Embracing the wounded landscape,
delicate shoots, resilient and proud
stand unbowed defying the ploy of warmongers.
Life blooms brazenly amidst the ruined choirs.

Each tender leaf stands as a new promise.
Each green tendril is a reminder of hope.
Each bold flutter takes an oath:
"No bullet can pierce the quiet rebellion
No war can stop the spirit stallion"
Little sapling declares its clarion call.

SHIELA DENISE SCOTT

Hope

I am yearning for a unity,
That combines a certain humanity,
And leaves no hate to suffocate this era in time,
I desire a delicacy,
A careful relevancy,
That admires its longing to be mine,
I daydream of expectancies,
Wanted, much needed leveraged reefs,
To float its way to the land in mind,
I have hoped for more than just a little,
And obtained a lot in this lifetime.

Craving Peace

My stomach rumbles each night,
No love in sight,
Only chaotic noise where I lay,
My headache gets worse,
As the feelings of tranquility goes away,
My heart aches,
Fears stake out the stillness,
That shall come,
Only if the tumultuous uproar,
Silence itself for more than one.

Unity of Hope

My life is in a bit of a mess,
But I have a better plan for that,
I reach out for hopes and explore dreams,
Journey with a detailed map,
Even though it's in a shambles,
A bit order less I must say,
I travel with my head held high,
And daydream others feel the same,
My aspirations hanker upon
    a deep-down feeling of trust,
Therefore, my hope aims to be felt for a union of us.

ANUPAMA SHAM BUDHRANI

Hope Keeps You Going

It's hope that keeps you going
It's hope that does the sowing
hope gives you wings
and satisfaction you get with things
hope keeps you upfront
gives you comfort in situations blunt
hope is the invisible strength
that gives your life a long length
hope helps you in every way
and allows you to stay
in every weather
come what may...
hope is the light at the end of the tunnel
hope gives you joys and happiness eternal
hope is the silver lining behind every cloud
and can circulate the world round
so giving hope to someone sad
is the only thing that adds
to the goodness in you
and to those that surround you
never lose hope
it helps you to cope
with any difficult situation
that is on the brink of a slope
and not elope

Hope

where there is hope
there are always dreams to cope
as life is stopless
you got to remain fearless

where there is hope to move on
time and dreams to fuel on
Air to travel and cap in
good luck and feelings to wrap in

as time goes by
Hope and dreams will stand high
in your chart of things
and the immense results they bring

Hope is the standing pillar
to make your life feel lighter
dreams take away your blues
and leave you behind with valuable clues

Hope Gives Social Possibilities

Hope gives you social possibilities
to remove the unwanted abnormalities
to educate the masses
to give them the power they ask

To fight for the downtrodden
To make them feel wanted
To help them live a respectable life
To help them overcome their strife

To remove social evils
To give people strength and feel
To give them hope and zeal
To give them time to heal

Hope allows you to go on
Hope allows you to move on
Hope gives you the right spark
to remove obstacles that are in the dark
Hope gives you a new path
to lead and follow your heart
To make things possible
and achieve societal change that is possible

NICOLE SMITH

Speak Up

I am working on a skill set
Using my voice
Not sitting by, quietly compliant
When words full of hate
Are spoken carelessly, effortlessly
Thinking no one will dare speak up
I am learning to use my voice
To stand up to racism, homophobia, bigotry
It is uncomfortable and hard
I can't sit in silence with my straight, white privilege
And not speak for those being repressed
It is cowardly.
I am working on using my voice
In opposition of oppressors
Instead of letting my safe silence
Make me complicit in hate.

Safe Space

I am a safe space
I will try my hardest
To protect you from harm
The world can be hard and cruel
I will help you weather the storms
That ebb and flow throughout life
I am a safe space
A place of understanding and love
I will stand beside you,
I will help you stand when you fall
(we all stumble, it happens)
I will believe in you,
When you struggle to believe in yourself
I will be gentle with your vulnerability
Let me be your safe space

Banned Books

Why are books banned?
Because marginalized groups
Might realize there are others
That understand, believe, have experienced
something similar
There is power
Power in knowing you aren't alone
You aren't a freak, an accident, a mistake
You aren't less than anyone else in existence
You don't deserve to be oppressed or repressed
History shouldn't be whitewashed
But told in vivid color
Your voice needs to be heard
Your history needs to be taught
Humanity should be held to a higher standard
Read banned books
Find acceptance and love for your fellow human
Celebrate our differences
Let go of outdated beliefs of
"How Things Should Be"

Let Everyone Be
Instead
Read banned books,
Discover what they want to keep hidden
Expand your horizon
Treat all humans with their deserved respect
Don't make different life experiences
A dirty secret

RONDA M. SMITH, PhD

How to Love a City?

How to love a city?
To love such a span of space?
A world with so much sin?

The question it was heavy –
    A daunting challenge I admit

Called upon for duty - A challenge the Lord imposed
To bring light and love into places –
    The darkness has enclosed

Shadows, corners, and lean-tos -
    Cover sadness, loss, and grief
People struggle in their shoes –
    In the high rises and in the streets

How to love a city? - I paused and looked around.
At all the many beautiful things -
    That make a place a town

A city brings together - People of all kinds
To service and provide, and - To educate their minds

A city is a place
Where dreams unite - yet streets divide
A city is a place
Where the lost - can surely hide

How to love a city? -
  With my hands, my feet, my heart?
Of all the ways to love, oh Lord...
  Where is it I should start?

The answer came - So swiftly,
Like a lightning bolt From rain!

Bring light into the darkness -
  Shine as for me, like sun
I tapped you to love this city –
  Love it like my Son!

Be a light into their darkness –
  Help them, find ways out of fear
Show them they are seen, and heard –
  Make people, welcome here.

Of all the things that you can do –
  With money, power and stuff
It starts - with truth in heart and mind –
  Show people how to love!

Freedom Can Wait

I stand before you
Strong - from a battle you can never know

I stand before you
Empowered - with beliefs from not so long ago

I stand before you
A symbol of freedom
But in some eyes, I'm hate?

What all has happened around me
For this to negate?

I came here legally
Pursuing all laws

But attitudes change -
And now ... I'm the cause?

I stand before you
Capable, Confident
An Educated American - with no discontent

But you...
Only see jealousy
Bitterness. Hate.

I came here for freedom.
I guess,
Freedom can wait.

Misunderstandings

Sensitive. Sensitivities.
In oh, so
many ways

Ambiguous. Ambiguities.
Watch your words
Don't participate.

Insecure. Insecurities.
We all feel them in our own ways.

Communicate. Clarify.
Words and feelings.
Glorify? Or vilify?

More so than ever in these days
We must try harder
To watch
what
WE say.

We can't know how the other will take it
Will they question it? Understate it?
Is it bigger than it was intended?
Did it strike nerves?
What has it penetrated?

Who is responsible for hurt feelings?
The one who speaks or the one who hears?
Blind I feel can be my reaching
I'll Keep trying though – it's taking years

LINDSAY SOBERANO WILSON

"Ten Cuidado" Is A Mother's Prayer

"Be safe," I say to my eldest son
as he heads out the door
and as I say it I wonder
if I still sound like me
or whether I said what it was I was thinking...

"Ten cuidado," mi abuela would say
to every one of her 11 children
as they headed out the door
in Tangiers and when they emigrated to Toronto.

"Ten cuidado" is a mother's prayer
a mother's wish
a mother's love
and even when all the *"ten cuidado"* in the world
doesn't amount to a shield of protection
at least and at last –
the heart knows what the heart knows.

VIVI SOJORHN

With a Friend the Old World Ends

Light and dark birds circle high,
An iridescent raven feasts where veils end.
Blood and guts are offerings now,
The hawk ascends without a sound.
Walking a curving road ahead,
Talking to Gwen about old dreams' death,
Heading down to flying birds' markers,
A liminal space, sunlight and dark,
The squirrel's hoarded energy is for sharing,
Old treasures given away without regret,
The raven stares at me and I stare back.
Fear circles like an omen's call,
But
Loyalty shakes the old world loose,
What rises from the time's end?
A Kosmic Egg takes shape in the dim,
Our beginning shimmering to behold.
What rises from time's end?
A new world is magical and sparkling
Light cracks through the shell.

LISA TOMEY-ZONNEVELD

Heaven on Earth

I believe that when nothing is said or done
about disparity
the soul cries

Love is all that we remember
when the angels call us home

I suppose that love is held in the soul

My soul is not worthy of this ascension
If he does not hold love for others

Then, there is the who we choose to emulate
Choices are ours to make
We have such freedoms
Only to be kept with love of fellow people

This causes pause for thought
Goals for heaven or a golden place
seem rather selfish
when love of others here on this earth
Is perhaps enough

Heaven on earth

I love that idea
Let's make it happen

LYNN WHITE

Into the Light

I'm living through the time
of night without end.
The time when everywhere is transformed
into the underworld.
When everywhere is transformed
into that dark place,
deathly dark.
Only the dark gods
and the creatures of death can live there,
those who need no further sustenance,
who gave up on the light above.
I won't give up.
I'm ready for the birth of a new day.
Ready for a pink dawn to rise
and break
full of possibilities,
as the light takes
over from the dark
and the day is born
again.
I shall follow the road towards the light,
and leave the dark behind,
again.

But I have found that the dark always follows.
Catches up with me, as if it were the past.
If I hurry maybe I'll escape it this time.
Maybe I'll catch the light
and hold on to it and
not let it break
again.

BIOS

Sarfraz Ahmed is an Amazon bestseller writer from the UK, who achieved success globally as a poet. His recent work includes *Pardon Me...You're Stepping on a Poet* and *The Ramblings of a Romantic Poet* (2023). In November 2024 he was nominated for a Pushcart Prize for his poem "Uncoil Me."

Rita Anderson, an internationally-published and award-winning writer, served as Dramatists Guild Regional Representative and as Faculty for Interlochen. She has had 100 productions and literary publications to include *Smith Kraus's BEST NEW 10-MINUTE PLAYS* four years running, but the highlight of her career so far was sharing a playwriting panel with Christopher Durang.

Nell Anthony is a Romance Ghost Writer for EGlobal Creative Publishing Limited in New York.
Primarily, she writes romance novels and poetry. She has an MFA in Creative writing from
Lesley University. She resides in Jacksonville, Florida. She is currently working on a romantic thriller that will debut in 2025.

Nanci Arvizu is an author, speaker, podcaster, publisher, and tech lover with nomadic dreams. Poetry and essays published at <u>NanciWrites on Substack</u> and in *A Safe and Brave Space* (2021), *Social Justice Inks* (2022), *Speak Magazine* (2022), and *Caring for Souls* (2022) and *Blood of My Enemies* (2020, fiction).

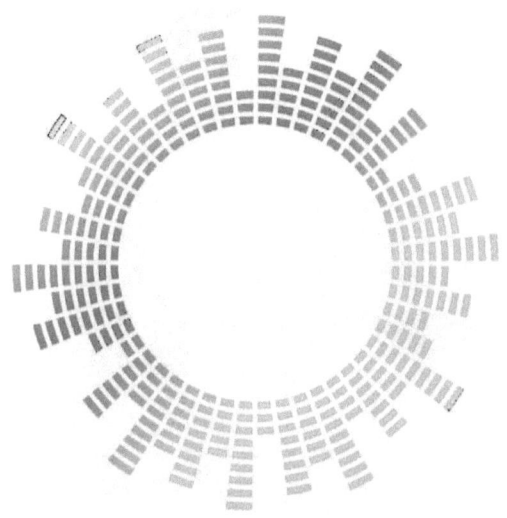

David Barnes lives in Weaverville, N.C. with his wife, Elaine. He began writing for publication in 2019 and has had works published in the quarterly Fine Lines Journal. East of the Web, Fiction on the Web, and Arzono Annual. Most of his pieces are short stories.

He's **Nayanjyoti Baruah**, a poet from Assam, India, who has a M.A. in English from Gauhati University. His poems have been appeared in state, national and international magazines and journals such as Rasa Literary Review, One Black Boy Like That Review, *The Journal of Undiscovered Poets, Libretto Magazine, Otherwise Engaged Journal, The Fiction Project, A Too Powerful Word, Necro Magazine, Open Door Magazine, Litterateur, AMASHIWII JOURNAL, Dovelyisi Magazine, D-Ample Magazine, The Chakkar Journal, Fasihi Magazine, The Defuncted Journal* etc. He's the co-author of 17 anthologies.

Roberta Batorsky is a poet, science journalist, and college educator. She has been writing poetry for about 5 years. She is in several online and in person poetry and fiction writing groups and is putting a poetry book together.

RobertaBatorsky_poetry (Instagram)

Thomas Beckwith is from Fort Lauderdale, Florida. He received a Bachelor of Arts in English with a concentration in Creative Writing from Virginia Tech. In his spare time, he enjoys watching sports and writing poetry. A quote that Thomas lives by is "Breathe to Survive, Strive to Succeed."

arlene s bice has published *Simply Put*, a collection of poetry. She received the Florence Poets Society Poet of Distinction Award and Annual Literary Oakley Hall Award. Her poems were performed in the Pandemic Blues at the Kirby Theatre directed by Fred Motley. She lives in Farmville, Virginia.

Susi Bocks - IWriteHer.com -
writer/author/poet/Editor of *The Short of It*, has
self-published two books and has many pieces
published in various anthologies and literary
magazines. She was a Pushcart Prize Nominee in
2021 for her piece "Sweet Embrace" featured in
Heart Beats Publisher: Prolific Pulse Press LLC.

Yasmin S Brown is an international bestselling co-author, Pushcart Prize poetry nominee, and certified life coach. Through innovation, she brings organizational health, communication, and trauma-informed awareness worldwide.

Yasmin S Brown's social media handles are Instagram and Facebook @yiryelements or visit her website at Yiry-Elements.

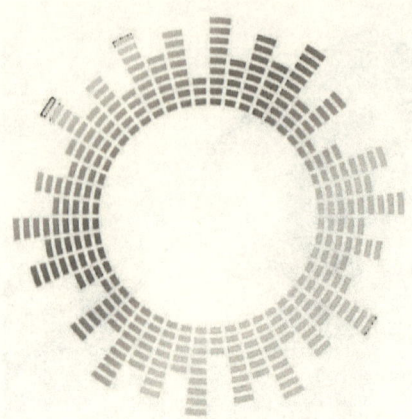

Stephen W. Buchanan enjoys writing poetry whenever the muse strikes. He posts under the pen name Muttado1sb, which is a play on Shakespeare's "Much Ado About Nothing" and a mutt being a blend of many things because his poetry is a blend of many nothings.

Joni Karen Caggiano, poet, photographer, and bestselling author, is a Best of The Net and three-time Pushcart nominee. Joni is a two-time winner of Publication of the Month and Socialite of the Year on Spillwords Press. Joni is an Adult Child of Alcoholics, rape survivor, environmentalist, and abuse education advocate.

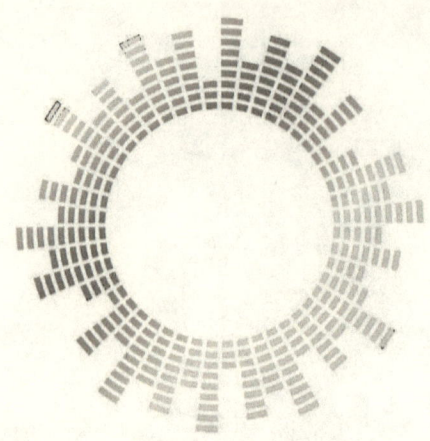

Vanessa Caraveo is an award-winning author, published poet, and artist whose literary work brings focus to various social issues that exist today. She has been published *in Literature Today Journal, The Poet Magazine, Latinidad Magazine, Poetrybay, Anacua Literary Arts Journal*, and in multiple anthologies throughout the years.

Theresa Carlie is a soul mate, dog mom, and little sister. She lives in Austin, TX but travels as much as possible, especially in August, when the Texas heat melts everything. She shares travel inspiration with fellow wanderers on her blog, HeyTraveler.com.

Cassa Bassa (Jia-Li Yang) is a Chinese-born Australian poet who captures the essence of human nature and emotions through poetry and micro-stories. Drawing inspiration from her surroundings, she weaves vivid reflections on life's depth and complexity. Her work can be found on her blog, flickerofthoughts.com

Carla M. Cherry authored six books: *Gnat Feathers and Butterfly Wings, Thirty Dollars and a Bowl of Soup, Honeysuckle Me, These Pearls Are Real, Stardust and Skin, May He Bless My Name* (iiPublishing), and three chapbooks, including *Sundays and Hot Buttered Rolls: A Granddaughter of Harlem Speaks* (Finishing Line Press).

Loralee Clark resides in Virginia; her Instagram is @make13experiment; her website is sites.google.com/view/loraleeclark. She has published, June 2025, *Solemnity Rites*, with Prolific Pulse Press LLC and has been published most recently in *Lucky Lizard, Nature of Our Times, Unearthed, Nebo, Choeofpleirn Press, Wingless Dreamer, Superpresent, and Thimble Literary Magazine*.

Lauren M. Clemmons is a published author based in Raleigh, North Carolina. Her essays, poetry, and fiction appear in anthologies, including TAF publications, and *Cadence, Life's Poetic Voices*, among others.

Candice Louisa Daquin is of French/Egyptian descent. She worked in publishing in Europe before immigrating to America to become a Psychotherapist. She edits for *Raw Earth Ink, Tint Journal, The Pine Cone Review, Parcham Literary Magazine*, and *Queer Ink*. Her last collection of poetry was *Tainted by the Same Counterfeit*.

Peter Devonald is a multi-award-winning writer based in Manchester, UK. Winner Loft Books 2024, Waltham Forest 2022, FofHCS and two HoH's, runner-up Shelley Memorial and N2tS 2024, Finalist Tickled Pink 2024, highly commended Hippocrates, Passionfruit Review, Saveas and Allingham. Nominations for Forward Prize and two BoN, widely-published/anthologised. Children's Bafta nominated.

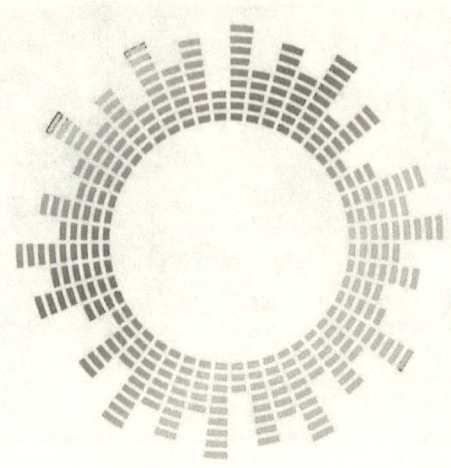

Aaliyah El-Amin lives in Prince George's County, MD, and is passionate about capturing the richness of human experience. Her works are featured in Maryland Bards and Neopoets anthologies, and she's a LexToday poetry finalist. She won "The Rhyme On" contest's funniest poem and is part of "Artists from Maryland."

Nolcha Fox's poems have been curated in print and online journals. Her poetry books are available on Amazon and Dancing Girl Press. Nominee for 2023, 2024, and 2025 Best of The Net. Nominee for 2023 and 2024 Pushcart Prize. Editor of Chewers by Masticadores. Co-Poetry Editor LatinosUSA.

Barbara Harris Leonhard is the author of three poetry collections. She is the Editor for MasticadoresUSA and FEED THE HOLY, and Co-Poetry Editor for LatinosUSA-English Edition. Her blog is Extraordinary Sunshine Weaver. She loves to drive to the Wetlands to count the geese and deer. She dreams of lasting peace.

Mark Andrew Heathcote is an adult learning difficulties support worker. His poems have been published in journals, magazines, and anthologies online and in print. He is from Manchester and resides in the UK. Mark is the author of *In Perpetuity* and *Back on Earth*, two books of poems published by Creative Talents Unleashed.

Duane L. Herrmann has carried baby kittens in his mouth, pet snakes, and conversations with owls, but careful not to anger them! Published in print and online, with degrees in education and history, despite a traumatic, abusive childhood embellished with dyslexia, ADHD; now compounded by cyclothymia, an anxiety disorder, and PTSD.

Tina Hudak is a writer-artist in the Washington, D.C. area has works included in The Library of Congress, Harvard Art Library and with small press publications in the U.S. and overseas. She is a nominee for the Pushcart Prize by The Garden of Neuro. Visit TinaOpines and A Blue Bunny Studio on Wordpress.

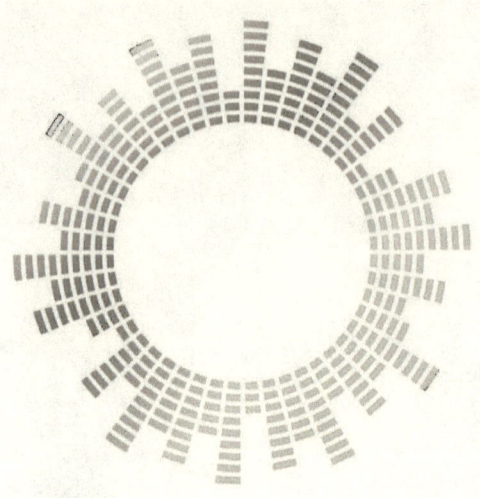

Dr. Michael Anthony Ingram, a Pushcart Prize nominee, believes "Poetry is a Lived Experience." His work confronts power, privilege, and oppression, and also interweaves themes of mental health awareness. As host of the acclaimed Quintessential Poetry podcast (www.qporytz.com), he creates spaces where spoken word meets social justice and healing.

Chyrel J. Jackson

Chyrel J. Jackson is a Literary luminary, 2025 poet Laureate and #1 Ranked Best Selling Amazon Author. Reared and raised in the South Suburbs outside Chicago. Black Literature influenced her writing. Chyrel Jackson writes in the spirit of her past great Literary ancestors.

Previously published works: *SistersRoc'N'Rhyme Presents Poems in the Key of Life, Mirrored Images* and *Different Sides of the Same Coin* Her writings: appear in multiple poetry Anthologies, Literary Journals, and International Global Magazines.

Zaneta V. Johns is a world-class author of three poetry collections and *What Matters Journal*. She has co-authored five international bestselling collaborative books and co-edited three poetry anthologies. Johns is an editor of *Fine Lines Journal* and Women Speakers Association Poet Laureate. Johns resides in Colorado, USA. ZanExpressions.com

Lin Marshall Brummels earned degrees from UNL and Syracuse University. Poems found - *Poet Lore, San Pedro River Review, Concho River Review, Oakwood, Plainsong, Nebraska Life*. Chapbooks, *Cottonwood Strong* and *Hard Times*, awarded Nebraska Book Award. Books, *A Quilted Landscape*, Scurfpea Publishing. Forthcoming, *The Last Yellow Rose*, Sandhills Press.

Danielle Martin is a former Caribbean Journalist and Copywriter who seeks to add the title of poet to her name. Danielle's work appears in several international print and online anthologies. Additionally, her own poetry collection, *Kissing Shadows: Caribbean Love Poems* is available on Amazon. Find her on FB @DanielleM

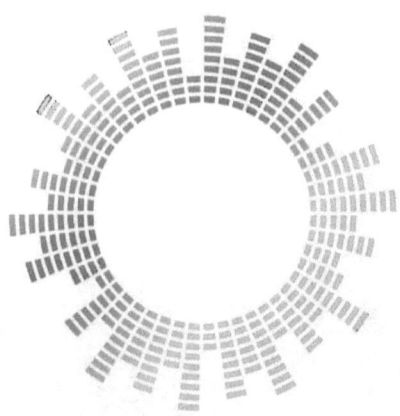

David Martin - is the founder and managing editor of *Fine Lines*, a non-profit quarterly journal that has published creative writing by "young authors of all ages" since 1992. All writers are welcome to submit their poetry, prose, photography, and artwork. This publication has printed work by authors from all 50 states and 100+ other countries. The website (www.finelines.org) has more information about submission guidelines and a sample journal to view. He has published two books of essays and poetry: *Facing the Blank Page* and *Little Birds with Broken Wings*.

Sarah Merritt Ryan is a poet, blogger, and memoirist. Her poetry has been published in anthologies by Whispering Angels Books, Prolific Pulse Press, PurpleStone Press, Fine Lines Journal, and Garden of Neuro Institute. She lives in North Carolina with her husband and son.

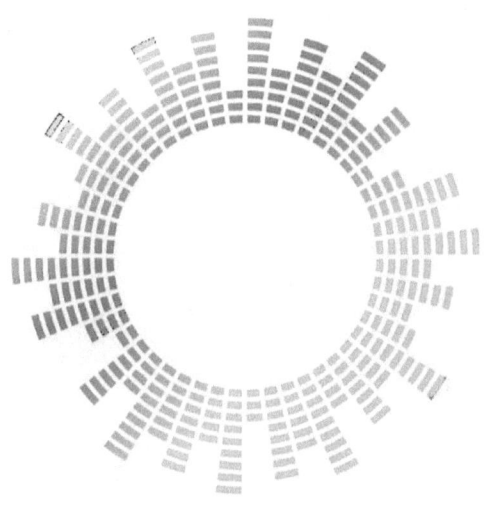

Author and photographer **Terri DeGezelle Michels** has published 64 children's non-fiction books, and a fiction picture book, *Simon of Cyrene, and Legend of the Easter Egg*.

Terri's passions include biking with her husband, spending time with family, and photographing the world around her. A proud native of Minnesota, the Land of 10,000 Lakes.

Karuna Mistry is a British writer of Indian ethnicity. He released his debut poetry book, *Sojourn: Transcending Seasons* (2024) via Amazon worldwide. His latest book release is *You-me-verse-all Hueman* (2025).

To date, he has over 90 poems published in almost 60 publications. Karuna is poetry editor for *Austur* magazine.

Instagram / Facebook: @karunamistrypoetry
Website: karunacreations.wordpress.com

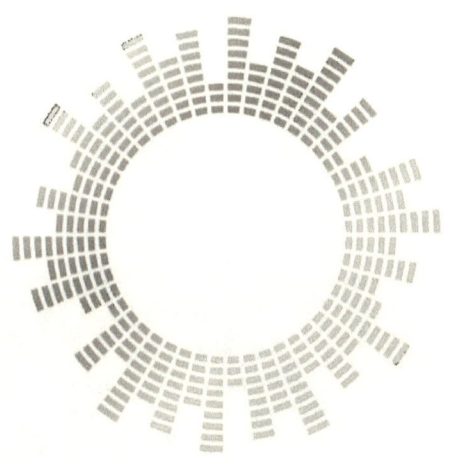

Davion Moore is a writer from Ohio. His passions include sports, poetry and documentaries. His poetry can be found in works such as the 2022 Poetry Marathon Anthology, the *Ohio Bards Anthology, Lost at 27: Musicians, Artists, Mortals and more*. He also has drabbles in various *Black Ink Fiction* projects.

Toluwanimi Adeniyi, pen name Nimitok, a poetic storyteller, weaving words into tapestries of culture and emotion. Guided by the belief that stories shape societies, and as one of the custodians of Art's voice, she channels creativity to the world through a ticking story every time.

Gypsie-Ami Offenbacher-Ferris lives in Southport, NC. Published in *Whisper's & Echoes, 50 Give or Take, Visual Verse, Spillwords* and in *Wounds I Healed*. Honorable Mentioned in *Tales from the Moonlit Path 2021 Halloween Challenge*. *Gypsie-Ami* has recently completed a chapbook merging her poetry and photography titled, *Reflections of a Woman's Life*.

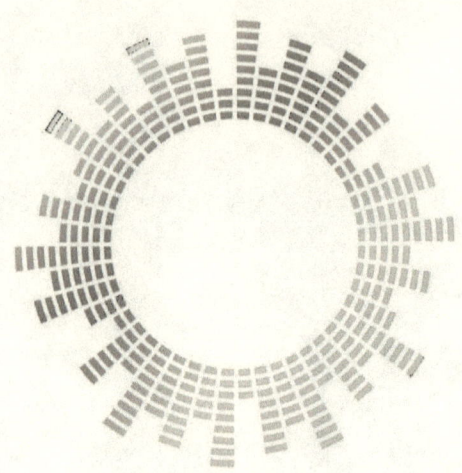

Dawn Pisturino's international publishing credits include poems, short stories, and articles. In 2024, she published four 5-star poetry collections. Three became a #1 Amazon New Release. All four ranked on Amazon Best Seller lists. She will release another poetry book and a children's book in 2025.

PoemsofCAMA
Ademide Christina Adelowo

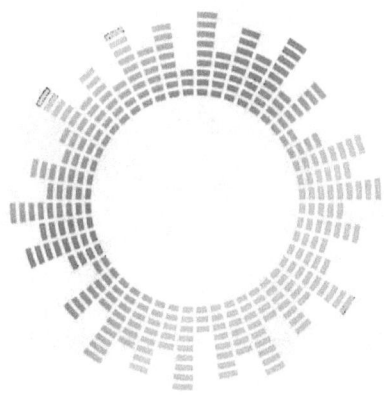

Ademide Christina Adelowo is a Nigerian who resides in Lagos, Nigeria. She is a graduate of English Language and Literary Studies. She has always loved to write poems ever since she was in high school. And many years of working in the media has spurred her to more poetic prowess.

Linette Rabsatt is a Virgin Islands poet with roots in the BVI and USVI. You can find her work in her Kindle book *Be Inspired*: *Poems by Linette Rabsatt*, in *Pulse Poetry Magazine*, on her blog, "Words of Ribbon," and on the *Visual Verse* and *Micromance Magazine* websites.

Ivan A. Salazar M., a passionate observer of life, hails from a land rich in poetic tradition, home to two Nobel Prize-winning poets. He crafts words with precision, creating poems that resonate with history and capture fleeting moments and eternal truths. His work reveals the raw beauty of the human condition, inviting readers to explore themselves. As a silent bard and published author, Salazar inspires and bridges cultures and hearts through the magic of his pen.

Munmun Samanta alias Sam was born in 1985 in rural India. An avid reader and writer by nature, she is a professional English language teacher and book reviewer. She loves to write short stories, essays, and poems. Her works have been published in various anthologies and magazines worldwide. Her debut short story collection *Yellow Chrysanthemum* was released in 2025.

Shiela Denise Scott award winning letter writer, finalist in quote contest, poetry finalist, photographer, and acrylic artist has been displayed in multiple magazines, anthologies, billboards, postcards, and canvas. Her multi-genre and mixed media style of works places her works in front of the eyes of art connoisseurs.

Anupama Sham Budhrani is a profound poet and author. She has completed her M.B.A. and Post graduation in Computer Applications. She has written three books: *A Collection of Poems, The Adventures of James Bond,* and *Poetry - A TASTE OF LIFE*. She hails from Visakhapatnam, Andhra Pradesh, India.

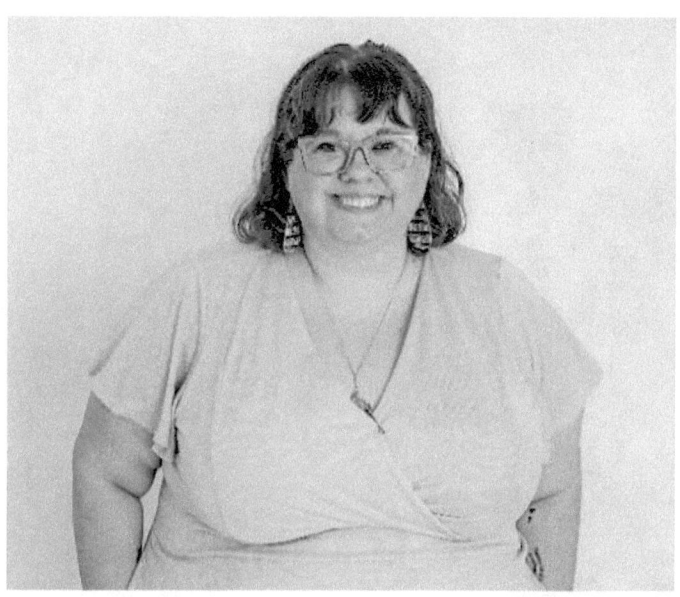

Nicole Smith is a published poet living outside Pittsburgh, PA with her husband, daughters, and pets. You can find her work in several anthologies. Follow her on socials; Momoetry blog on WordPress, facebook.com/momoetry or Instagram @Momoetry22.

Ronda M. Smith, PhD is a published author and poet, an actor, advocate, inspiring educator, speaker, entrepreneur and world traveler. She earns her living as a professor of entrepreneurship, creativity, positive applied psychology and organizational behavior.

Lindsay Soberano Wilson is a teacher and author. "The Japanese Red Maple" from her debut poetry collection *Hoods of Motherhood* (Prolific Pulse Press, 2023) was nominated for a Pushcart Prize. *Breaking Up With the Cobalt Blues: Poems For Healing* (Prolific Pulse Press, 2024), features visual and lyrical poems that find peace in painful, messy, shameful parts of life unearthed at inconvenient times. She is a contributing writer to the anthology *Cadence: Life's Poetic Rhythms*; (Prolific Pulse Press LLC, (2024), which was a Finalist in the American Writing Awards. *Casa de mi Corazon: A Travel Journal* explores how her Canadian Jewish identity was shaped by travel (2021).

Vivi Sojorhn is a poet, tarot master, and philosopher weaving light, shadow, and story into every line. Her work bends time, decoding symbols, unearthing mystic secrets, and dreaming futures shimmering with possibility. Published in Work by Prolific Pulse Press LLC, she believes poetry is both starmap and spell for the wandering soul.

Lisa Tomey-Zonneveld is the founder and manager of Prolific Pulse Press LLC and a widely published poet and writer. She is the editor of numerous anthologies and is an editor for *Fine Lines Journal*. Tomey-Zonneveld is the Poet Laureate Emeritus of Garden of Neuro Institute and resides in North Carolina.

ProlificPulse.com

Blog: ProlificPulse.blog

Lynn White lives in north Wales. Her work is influenced by issues of social justice and events, places and people she has known or imagined. She is especially interested in exploring the boundaries of dream, fantasy and reality.

https://lynnwhitepoetry.blogspot.com and

https://www.facebook.com/Lynn-White-Poetry-1603675983213077/

Social Commentary from the Perspective of Community, Race, Rage, Social Injustice

A Collaboration by Chyrel J. Jackson, Melissa Lemay, Danielle Martin, Zaneta V. Johns, and Lisa Tomey-Zonneveld

I am finally out of the kitchen.
Educated, well-spoken,
still treated like a white man's token.

Is it possible to buy produce without rage?
Whose hands picked these apples, harvested
bananas,
  plucked cabbage
are the same hands that many a man
  is not willing to shake.
They say it's all relative.
I am paused to think, we are all
  some kind of relative
Or am I wrong?

My stepfather laughed
As he called Black people n—
His words abhorrent to my
Young ears
I don't belong there
White girl,
You don't belong here
Not welcome anywhere.

Colour coded locks drenched in blood,
bind me to a past that can never be shook
as I still hear the faint jingle jangle of keys,
held by new, soft, white hands of old,
hiding within the bosom of ignorance,
ancestors, well nourished
and cradled by bruised and beaten,
black, wet nurses.

America's toxic red, privileged white
          and blatant blue climate
Was never kind to its Black citizens
Our hearts of gold
          and undisputable works
Reflect pure allegiance to this land.

Women Poets SHINE Community

The Women Speakers Association's global gathering place for women poets

The Women Speakers Association (WSA) is a global network supporting women in over 120 countries, across six continents. WSA Founder Gail Watson and I launched the Women Poets SHINE Community on Facebook in 2024. As WSA Poet Laureate and leader of this platform, I created the Poet Success Plan, a valuable tool to assist creatives on their poetic journey. You may access this free resource at http://www.poetsuccessplan.com/ or use the QR code below.

To learn more about WSA, visit WomenSpeakersAssociation.com

Zaneta V. Johns, WSA Poet Laureate

Garden of Neuro Publishing

Submissions are accepted year round.

Go to FineLines.org for submission guidelines.

To all the contributors:

It takes a lot of heart
and soul to write poetry
so deep and truthful.

We see this in every
single anthology.

We are grateful for all
you do to continue to
offer hope in poetry.

www.ingramcontent.com/pod-product-compliance
Lightning Source LLC
Chambersburg PA
CBHW021622120626
46545CB00001B/362